Weaving Strong Leaders

How Leaders
Grow Down, Grow Up, and Grow Together

BOB DALE *and* BILL WILSON

© 2016
Published in the United States by Nurturing Faith Inc., Macon GA,
www.nurturingfaith.net.

Library of Congress Cataloging-in-Publication Data is available.

ISBN 978-1-63528-000-5

*Healthy Church Resources are provided by the Center for Healthy Churches
(chchurches.org) in collaboration with Nurturing Faith Publishing (nurturingfaith.net).*

"My single disappointment with this book is that it wasn't written 30 years ago. To all of us who are drowning in books about 'how to do such and such' and '10 steps to this and that,' Bob Dale and Bill Wilson have issued a life preserver. Reading this book was for me a profoundly spiritual experience."
—*Julie Pennington-Russell, Pastor, The First Baptist Church of the City of Washington, D.C.*

"This book is an essential field guide for anyone who is serious about personal transformation as a leader. Bob Dale and Bill Wilson are thoughtful and seasoned guides in this journey, marking out a path for such a pilgrimage that is grounded in God's story and shaped by our own experiences."
—*Jayne Hugo Davis, Associate Pastor – Discipleship, First Baptist Church, Wilmington, N.C.*

"Reading this book is like having a series of conversations with wise friends, skilled leaders, and caring mentors. Bob Dale and Bill Wilson weave together solid scriptural and theological reflection, keen insight into the human journey, broad awareness of leadership theories, and abundant practical experience to provide a rich resource for leaders' personal and professional growth."
—*Guy Sayles, Assistant Professor of Religion, Mars Hill University*

"It is fitting that a leadership book with the guiding image of 'weaving' is a product of two authors who bring vast experience and wisdom in the area of leadership in the church. Bob Dale and Bill Wilson weave together their personal stories, decades of experiences, and key insights that form an outstanding guide for church leaders today. Their description of the different life stages of a leader who 'grows up' into personal maturity will make this book an outstanding resource for leaders of all ages and experience levels. I highly recommend it and will plan to use it in the seminary leadership course I teach."
—*David Hull, Southeast Coordinator, Center for Healthy Churches;*
Adjunct Professor, McAfee School of Theology of Mercer University

"From two of the best leadership teachers and coaches comes this personal and practical handbook on leadership development and maturity. Rather than a 'how to' book on practices, this is a 'who we are' book from the practitioners of leadership. It focuses on a theology and trajectory for leaders and is full of biblical examples. It is highly readable with personal stories, dialogue between the authors, and probing questions for personal reflection. I heartily recommend it."
—*Craig Sherouse, Senior Pastor, Second Baptist Church, Richmond, Va.*

"I've known Bob Dale since my seminary days in the mid-1980s, and Bill Wilson since I was a young pastor. Both are leaders among leaders. They are rare leaders who not only practice leadership with excellence, but also can teach others to lead. This book brings old and new wisdom to the topic of leadership, specifically Christian leadership. Emerging leaders and established leaders will find it to be a valuable addition to their library and their leadership."
—*Larry Hovis, Executive Coordinator, Cooperative Baptist Fellowship of North Carolina*

"The leader's journey is long and arduous and ought not to be taken alone. In this book Bob Dale and Bill Wilson prove themselves faithful guides. It is a reminder that what our churches most desperately need right now cannot be downloaded from the internet, but must instead be woven into the soul."
—*Ryon Price, Senior Pastor, Second Baptist Church, Lubbock, Texas*

"Leaders may be born, but leadership is crafted. Effective and lasting leaders learn to take the successes, disappointments, and insights from others along with their own journey in Christ and weave them together into a comprehensive understanding of their calling and their culture. Bob Dale and Bill Wilson, both effective leaders in their respective fields, have given us a realistic understanding of how leadership comes together in our lives and then how our new understanding of leadership can best be used in our communities. Both challenging and affirming, Dale and Wilson have given us a readable and realistic understanding of how authentic leadership is woven together in our lives."

—*Mike Glenn, Senior Pastor, Brentwood Baptist Church, Brentwood, Tenn.*

"Bill and Bob have turned the leadership art and skill inside out. Focusing on the source of leadership rather than the 'what' and 'how' of leadership, they reveal the blind spot of most leadership paradigms: the person of the leader. Using their personal narratives, Bill and Bob deepen the well from which authentic leadership is drawn."

—*Steven N. Scoggin, Assistant Vice-President, CareNet and Behavioral Health, Assistant Professor in Psychiatry and Behavioral Medicine, Wake Forest University Baptist Medical Center*

"This book is the kind of resource church staff, leadership teams, and all youth and young adults should read for the profound insights it contains. Bob Dale is a masterful storyteller of his life pilgrimage around the framework of the tapestry of life development. He can take a concept and illustrate it with a narrative in amazing ways. Equally helpful are the consultant/coaching insights of Bill Wilson as he applies concepts and stories to the realities of congregational life. Buy a copy for each leader in your church, whatever his or her age!"

—*Larry L. McSwain, Professor of Leadership, Retired, McAfee School of Theology*

"Buy, read, reflect upon, return to, and share this book. Dale and Wilson reframe Christian leadership, freeing it from 'copycatting' secular techniques and turning it toward core developmental, theological, community, and heritage concerns. Seasoned and developing congregational leaders will find what they need here."

—*Michael A. Smith, Senior Pastor, Central Baptist Church of Fountain City, Knoxville, Tenn.*

"While guiding the reader on a reflective journey to determine our affinity to 'mystery or mechanics,' the authors share personal journeys of success, struggle, failure, and a time of cultivating one's soul, calling, and professional identity. Not only do they help us explore the deeper why's of leadership, but they also challenge us to keep growing and mining truths in the context of today's world. Without minimizing the growing diversity of our culture and the steep challenges of ministry in today's world, the authors provide biblical and historical frameworks and landmarks to assist the leader's journey of self-awareness, spiritual and relational growth, and effectiveness. This is a great book for seminary students, pastors, and lay leaders."

—*Edward Hammett, President, Transforming Solutions*

"The legacy and wisdom of Bill Wilson and Bob Dale shine through in this book. They effectively recognize that leadership is a lifelong pilgrimage where leaders exhibit different threads as they weave their lives and ministry. This is a book to read not once, but several times along your journey as a lifelong leader. Keep it close by."

—*George Bullard, Leadership Consultant/Coach, The Columbia Partnership, FaithSoaring Churches Learning Community*

Contents

Dedicated to all leaders
who are ready to
grow down, grow up, and grow together

Acknowledgments

We owe our leadership trajectories to the influences of many others—parents and families, spouses and friends, teachers and mentors, critics and truth-tellers. We thank each and all of them.

In the pages that follow we'll weave threads from our personal and professional stories. In the process we'll trace our leadership stories that give context and make meaning for us. Hopefully these stories will give guidance to you, too. These varied threads have woven themselves together into the stories we live.

Writing this book became a weaving process, with each of us contributing different parts. Bob drafted Parts 1 and 2. Bill drafted Part 3 and "The Consultant's Loom" commentaries.

The leader theology in Part 1 "grew down" when Bob taught a seminary readings course with Rose Mary Stewart on how Trinitarian theology undergirds the work of leaders.

The maturity pilgrimages for leaders in Part 2 "grew up" from a family history Bob wrote with his wife Carrie for their own children.

In Part 3, the applications of how teams and clusters of leaders "grew together" emerged from Bill's consulting ministry. The result is an actual weaving of leadership.

Both of us have had varied ministries. We've served as pastors, teachers, lay leaders, volunteers, consultants, counselors, and coaches. We've led new church starts and guided transitions in older ministries. We've served on boards for divinity schools, pastoral counseling centers, newspapers, and denominational groups.

We've both succeeded and failed. We've both dusted ourselves off and tried again. We've both learned on the fly.

So, we apologize in advance for our biographical stories in these pages. Our stories are the ones we know and understand best. We've lived them inside out—warts and all. Over time, God, as weaver of our lives and stories, has formed us for his work.

Now, we move on to those stories of growing up, growing down, and growing together.

Bob Dale
Bill Wilson

Preface
Selecting Leadership's Threads

Welcome to the inner lives of leaders. Current leadership literature is more apt to feature practices than practitioners—what leaders do rather than who leaders are. Much of today's leadership literature seems to assume leaders burst forth ready to lead with little introspection or no struggle.

We know better. Our best leaders are anchored in clear values and considered beliefs. They have grown down. And, our best leaders have cultivated their own maturity. They have grown up and are comfortable in their skins. Growing down, growing up: In the pages ahead we trace and weave together these two master threads.

Lessons from the Loom

Our lives, as effective leaders, are woven threads. What we believe, how we mature, the ways we work together: All are related.

Navajo weavers, gifted artisans who craft beautiful garments and durable rugs, have much to teach church leaders. These weavers create their unique art with both traditional and mystical methods.

Like other weavers, Navajos use the vertical threads, or the "warp," to establish strong and lasting foundations. Then they interlace the horizontal design threads, or the "woof," to feature texture and beauty.

Strength and beauty: By selecting and using these two basic threads, Navajo crafters make weavings that both endure and inspire. Like weavers, church leaders understand the fundamental importance of combining anchoring strengths with beautiful practicality.

Faith and Flaws

For leaders of faith there's an intriguing and mystical element in Navajo woven products. In each item the Navajo weavers include a deliberate flaw—an escape portal for any evil that's been accidentally trapped by the threads. That makes deep sense to those of us who lead. We recognize the constant tug-of-war between good and evil inside us and within our faith communities. We want evil on the outside and good on the inside of our leadership efforts.

When my son, Cass Dale, professed his faith in Christ back in the mid-1980s, our pastor asked what he had decided. Cass asked the pastor if he'd seen the *Star Wars* movie, and he discovered the pastor knew that story. Cass said, "That's my story too. There's a battle between good and evil in the world. I'm joining the side of good."

More perhaps than pacesetters without exposure to theology, congregational leaders know that faith and flaws coexist in our own lives. No one is perfect, including leaders, so we cultivate faith and maturity constantly—to help us see, face, and overcome our flaws. We acknowledge our shortcomings, lean on God's grace, and try to live and lead with humility. We rely on our faith to provide a foundation for us and to open futures to us.

Threads for the Future

The fabric of Christian leadership weaves two threads together in practice: (1) faith—deepening, transforming belief; and (2) maturity—stabilizing, unfolding selfhood.

We believe the strongest church leaders are belief-based. With a theological foundation, we are anchored against storms. We have a place to stand. When we're comfortable with and confident in our basic beliefs and values, our behaviors flow consistently from a solid faith.

We believe the best church leaders are mature and well-defined. Mature leaders know where we begin and end. We're clear about "me" and "not me." Secure and anchored egos aren't under threat or at risk. Effective leaders have strong, not big, egos. And, our most mature church leaders play well with others. We gladly blend and match our strengths and experiences with others' talents and backgrounds.

These two themes—believing and maturing—are threads interwoven throughout this book. At the end we'll suggest how leader teams are woven together to make the most of believing and maturing. Are you ready to weave your life as a leader?

Introduction

Weaving Leaders and Lives

L eaders are on a personal and professional pilgrimage, deepening theology and maturity. It's a lifelong journey. Our life's threads continue to be woven together.

Life is an uneven journey. Over our lifespan we lurch along between seasons of stability and times of change.[1] We oscillate back and forth, around and around. Sometimes change moves smoothly for us; on other occasions, change becomes an extremely bumpy ride. The rhythms of our lives often remind us of the airline pilot's description of commercial flying: hours and hours of sleep-inducing tedium punctuated by moments of sheer terror.

Growing our beliefs and cultivating our maturity are two of life's unending processes. Over time we fold our discoveries into the fabric of our lives. We choose what to keep and what to jettison. We decide how to be stewards of our deeper resources, to cultivate and use them. We apply life's lessons. As we mature in soul and self, our identity and values become steadying anchors for us:

- We find faith and persistently grow deeper in it.
- We learn whether our faith is a buoying resource or a guilt-inducer. (Then we cooperate with God in developing a positive faith that moors us.)
- We learn how we were shaped and launched by our families and mentors.
- We discover how to put success and failure into balanced perspective.
- We find how to grace ourselves with the gift of second chances.
- We learn how to step back and mull over what has happened and to use what's happening around us now.
- We discover whether our family and friends are encouraging cheerleaders or poisonous detractors. (Then we choose our healthiest personal and professional communities as centers for growth and depth.)
- We welcome God's love in our lives and risk being made new daily.

The good news is that faith and maturity tend to deepen as our lives unfold. Our hope is to grow up and down as we go along. We find faith and maturity, and, with God's help, they find us. Faith and maturity often deepen and unfold layer by layer—first struggling toward self-discovery, next surviving and growing, then finding significant legacy, and finally sharing life's gifts by paying and praying it forward.[2]

Life at the Loom

Life places a variety of "challenge threads" on faith-and-maturity's loom. These hurdles etch lines in our faces, add gray to our hair, and leave stretch marks and scars on our bodies. But these challenges also help us grow up and down. Broken bones knit stronger at the fracture points than beforehand. Where souls and selves are on the line, pain brings gains.

The pilgrimage toward deeper faith and stronger maturity is well documented in Scripture. Profound pilgrimages leave marks, though. Jacob limped after his wrestling match with an angel (Gen. 32:31). Disbelief during the wilderness wandering cost the lives of an entire generation (Num. 14:23). Ruth's care for her mourning mother-in-law created a redemptive lineage (Ruth 1:16-17, 4:13-17). The Damascus Road blinded Paul and sent him to Arabia to sort out his confusion (Gal. 1:15-17). In each case, faith and maturity grew as challenges were faced squarely.

With growing faith, these spiritual pacesetters discovered how to listen, when to slow down and discern, how to recover after being crushed, and how to find themselves after being lost. Hardship is often a pathway to peace and productivity.

Growing Down, Growing Up

Let's chart our growth pilgrimage's twists and turns. *As leaders we grow in faith and maturity when we weave our life stories into a larger faith story*, when we weave our life's brokenness into healed places, and when we weave our life's opposites into conversations with each other.

Leaders of faith and with maturity know who we are, understand where we begin and end, and sense when to say yes and no (Matt. 6:37). Our inner compass, our guidance system of faith and identity, orients and anchors us. We become clearly defined. That self-definition is the product of patiently weaving self and soul together, discovering the interplay of our unique stories with God's big story.

You and I tell the stories of our lives. These stories are multilayered and can be tangled. We recall personal incidents. These little stories explain a bit about us, can entertain others, and create some connections to others.

We then begin to detect patterns in and between our stories. Now we see larger meanings and connections across our life's seemingly random events. Over time those bigger stories of family and faith merge and give meaning to our lives. They begin to "tell us." These stories tell who we are, what we're about, and where we're heading. Instead of a handful of random stories, we now have a thread that organizes life into a meaningful narrative.

We then realize there's an overarching story that really explains us. Faith expands and grounds our story. We see the Bible as the biggest story of all,[3] the story of redemption. From Genesis to Revelation, Scripture tells us the big story of how God has acted mightily to draw us into relationship with him.

We finally move inside God's story. When we enter fully into the Christian life, this redemption story wraps around us and becomes our story. In fact, when we live inside the salvation narrative and claim it as ours, we can't imagine ourselves in any other story. It defines us, explaining us in profound ways. We've been found, called, and sent out to make a redemptive difference in the world.

Inside God's story we find surprises. Our "assumptive worlds"—those ideas we have always accepted as true and never examined—now float out of the mist and we recognize them. We Photoshop the old pictures in our heads—our assumptions about the world—so we can see new worlds in new ways. Our "truth" expands. Now we realize that becoming a disciple is a life-long process of discovery and risk-taking. We update our thinking and grow.

We've all been in the wrong place at the wrong time when life unfairly slapped our faces. Or, we've been in the right place at the right time when life gave us an undeserved pat on the back. In other words, we have realized that life's penalties and rewards are often out of our personal control. We've been there and done that, haven't we?

For good or ill, *we find ourselves caught up in life's surprises and breakage.* Resilience from our faith and maturity becomes the swing vote in these circumstances. Ultimately, it's not what happens to us that matters most. It's what we do with what happens to us that makes the crucial difference and measures our faith and maturity. Responding to events beyond our control gives us a chance to grow down and up. Leaders with faith and maturity are agile enough to deal with life's accidents and mistakes.

In the midst of unchosen turning points we make trade-offs and trade-ups. We try to exchange losses for gains, grudges for forgiveness, blind spots for insights, complexities for simple elegance, and hurts for healings. We discover new parts of our lives and determine that some are outmoded or dysfunctional. In the face of those realities we can trade up to more mature choices for us at our current life stage.

How we deal with turning points and trade-ups is a basic clue to our faith and maturity levels. Picking up the loose, broken threads of life and weaving them back together helps us grow. They strengthen us for the future. Mature judgment often emerges from the debris of immature judgment.

Thinking and acting in both/and fashion is one mark of faith and maturity. Holding opposing alternatives is a basic part of moving successfully through cycles of stability and change.[4] When we're overwhelmed by life, we freeze internally. To unthaw our thinking and to move ahead, we try to see life as a whole, a process that's always in transition. We try to suspend our options and patiently sort out possibilities. We integrate and enrich our problem-solving approaches.

Some understandings of human development note that we focus on discovering our inner opposites during the first half of our lives. Then we grow toward the emotional middle between our opposites during our second half of life. That process of "moving to the middle" helps us balance our best selves and souls.

Once we've thawed the poles of our lives, we can then turn to our futures. Theologically, it's an act of faith to describe our futures in plurals. Redemption is always expansive. There's so much more to the world than we first see or suspect. God has doors—doors beyond our imagining—already open and waiting for us. Past is prelude, present is rehearsal, and our futures are waiting for us to see and seize them.

Now the leadership weaving adventure begins.

Mooring Firmly on Theological Beliefs

Christians are moored by theological beliefs, the lengthwise threads in leadership tapestries. In this book we affirm a Trinitarian approach to leaders' transformation—centering in the kingdom of God, modeling Jesus' ways of relating to others, and relying on the Holy Spirit's power.

God's kingdom serves as an anchor and a guide for faith leaders. Jesus' leader patterns show faith leaders how to relate and proceed. The Holy Spirit empowers faith leaders to move ahead creatively. How is our strength rooted in the redemptive work of the Trinity?

Maturing Ourselves Stage-by-Stage

Kierkegaard's classic observation is true: we live our lives forward and then understand them backwards. That's the intention for the maturity section of this book, the crosswise threads in this leadership tapestry. How do our adult lives unfold stage-by-stage? We examine several questions:

☐ How do we mature as people, persons of faith, and leaders?
☐ How do we let our flaws escape and then welcome depth and clarity in their place?

As life stages run their course, we can check to see what we've mastered and where gaps remain in our maturation processes. Each decade contains distinctive challenges and offers rich opportunities. In broad strokes we can chart the spiritual journey toward maturity and leadership as follows:

☐ Teen years and earlier—Dream and discover.
☐ 20s—Explore and expand.
☐ 30s—Climb and achieve.
☐ 40s—Bridge and redefine.
☐ 50s—Contribute and leave a legacy.
☐ 60s—Invest in others and in our own futures.
☐ 70s and beyond—"Sage" and pay it forward.

Each decade, then, becomes an occasion to learn, mature, believe, and move ahead with confidence. At each stage we can evaluate how our pilgrimage toward maturity is progressing and working for or against us.

Look to the past. We can look back upstream to what has gone before. We can cultivate what we've inherited from others and what we've experienced in life that's healthy and reliable. At the same time we can let go of histories and habits that no longer serve us well. We can ask ourselves:

☐ What life, faith, and leader stages have I mastered already?
☐ What's still left for me to learn as I mature more?

Look at the present. We can look into the mainstream and check where we are in the present moment. We can deepen and build on sturdy foundations. From that base we can use yesterday and today as a launch pad toward tomorrow. We can ask ourselves:

☐   Where am I grown up now?
☐   What life lessons must I learn now on the fly?
☐   What learning gaps must I let bridge my life, faith, and leadership?

Look to the future. We can look downstream toward the future and antici-
pate where our paths lead. As we mature more fully, we can risk our futures
with confidence. We can ask ourselves:

☐   What's next for me in life, faith, and leadership?
☐   What resources am I stewarding?

Creating Leader Teams

We'll complete our leadership tapestry with a congregational application—by
describing leaders in different roles, with varying experience levels, and with a
variety of gifts. We'll talk about the mix and blend of four leadership roles—
the NOW, NEW, NEXT, and NEAR leaders.

NOW leaders are in the midst of the fray. NEW leaders are just moving
into the arena. NEXT leaders are poised on the sidelines and preparing for
larger service. NEAR leaders have broad experience and walk alongside the
NOW, NEW, and NEXT leaders as coaches and guides to provide perspective.

It takes creative blends of all four roles to lead congregations and faith
organizations well. The African proverb says wisely: "If you want to go fast,
go alone. If you want to go far, go together."

The Consultant's Loom

As we launch this grand adventure of learning about leadership, I remember
an early lesson that continues to impact me as I navigate my season of investing in others and paying forward all the gifts I have been fortunate enough
to receive.

Early in my ministry I was infatuated with and captured by methods.
With a full and demanding personal and professional schedule, I found myself
constantly under pressure to deliver programs and services to a demanding
congregation. Taking the time to dig deep and think hard about ministry
seemed like a luxury, and so I settled for adopting the work of others. It wasn't
so much plagiarizing as it was abdicating the task of study and thoughtful
reflection. I loved reading sermons and leadership books, and I often attended
conferences to listen to profound and inspiring thought leaders.

Rather than develop my own philosophy or theology of ministry, I simply shopped around for good ideas, creative methodologies, and best practices. Bringing them home, I would import them into my ministry situation and assume that just bringing the words to a group or the ideas to a team meant I had done my job.

Quickly I learned how naïve I was. Ideas that worked elsewhere fizzled in my setting. Sermon ideas that came from others came off as inauthentic when I tried to preach them. My array of splendid methods offered without an underlying thoughtfulness produced little of significance. In the end I felt shallow and inauthentic. The public life of ministry became confusing and conflicted for me. Some of my favorite role models flamed out and proved unreliable. Exasperated, I turned away from what had worked for others and started the hard journey of self-discovery.

I found my inspiration in horticulture. Roots come first, before fruit. Writers such as Bob Dale, Stephen Covey, and Ed Friedman showed me how to go below the surface and do this arduous work of foundation-building before (and while) living the public side of leadership. If we can help you do the same, we will all be better for it. So, put aside what works for others and allow God to lead you on a path toward self-discovery. What you will find there will become your doorway to a life of meaning and significance.

The Art and Craft of Leader Weaving

This book explores leaders' theology and maturity, leaders' matches and mobilizing actions. These weavings open us to God's futures. They encourage us to cultivate self and soul, to share our gifts and pool our strengths with other leaders. Read on with some basic questions and one practical application in mind:

- [ ] How can we grow theologically grounded leaders?
- [ ] How can we map the growth process of stronger, more mature leaders?
- [ ] How can we understand leaders' roles?
- [ ] How can we create teams for the health and vitality of our congregations?

Are you ready to begin weaving your leader life and the leader potential of others?

Notes

[1] Frederic M. Hudson, *The Adult Years: Mastering the Art of Self-Renewal* (San Francisco: Jossey-Bass, 1991).

[2] Bob Buford, *Finishing Well: What People Who Really Live Do Differently!* (Nashville: Integrity Publishers, 2004), 13-14.

[3] Craig G. Bartholomew and Michael W. Goheen, *The Drama of Scripture: Finding Our Place in the Biblical Story* (Grand Rapids: Baker Academic, 2004).

[4] Roger Martin, *The Opposable Mind: How Successful Leaders Win Through Integrative Thinking* (Boston: Harvard Business School Press, 2007).

PART 1

Threading the Loom
Identifying Our Theology for Leadership

Today's leaders face a watershed choice: mystery or mechanics. We're products of a mechanistic culture, but the mystery of our ancient-future worldview offers a key correction. Without a theological foundation, leadership is just another job.

But when we serve the "Other" with a sense of awe, the holy mystery of leadership emerges. Remember that the Hebrews of the Old Testament did not use God's name for fear it would shrink and trivialize our Creator, Judge, and Redeemer. In that spirit we root leadership in the mysteries of God's Trinitarian nature.

Remember the Navajo weavers? To create tapestries, they use two sets of threads: (1) lengthwise threads for strength and (2) crosswise threads for texture and beauty. Fabrics aren't complete, sturdy, or interesting until both sets of threads are intertwined.

Leaders weave together two sets of threads too: (1) theology for strength and (2) maturity for texture and beauty. Ask yourself:

☐ As a Christian leader, what's my strong theological thread?
☐ As a Christian leader, how mature am I for my leadership opportunities?

Putting First Threads First
Leading from the Master Threads

Remember that leadership is an active faith role, a practice. Leaders put on our work gloves and live out our faith concretely. We find our "why," and then we ask "what now." A faith practice calls for a practical, working faith.

What if we led from a master thread, a theological North Star? Not just any old set of directions, not just some "tricks of the trade" or a changing list of best practices, but something lasting and eternal. Something solid and dependable. Something that sets a clear trajectory. What if a theological master thread—a set of belief-based behaviors—guided and kept us on course?

Visible Values, Anchored Actions

The best leaders rely on a stance, an orientation to build on and to guide us. That resource is our "strength thread." Theology makes our values visible and anchors our actions.

We religious leaders haven't always worked from a theological base. Leadership, as a formal academic discipline, is less than a century old and emerged from secular studies. Too often, religious leaders have adopted whatever approach is new and different, with little regard for reliable foundations.

I began studying leadership as a professional discipline with Consultant Trainers Southwest in 1968 in Texas. Then I began teaching the practice of congregational leadership formally in 1973 as a Nashville-based traveling consultant-teacher for Baptist audiences. Later, in 1977, I moved into the classroom as a seminary professor in North Carolina to teach pastoral leadership, the first pastoral leadership professor in the Baptist world. Finally, I founded a leadership center for Virginia Baptists and taught leaders in that setting from 1989 until 2009.

Since there were no pastoral leadership classes in my seminary training, I first learned leadership from sports, business, and military sources—and then added belief-based ones. As a result, I became a good mimic of the leadership methods of high-profile sports coaches, successful business executives, and famous military leaders. Then, when I taught leadership to church leaders, I simply "baptized" and translated the views and practices of those well-known secular leaders.

As a leader and teacher of leaders, I now see that I sometimes settled for second best. "How" we led wasn't my primary blind spot. From an activist denomination we found plenty of ways to advance our causes. "Why" we led was our weak point. We were too pragmatic. If it worked, we did it without thinking theologically. We didn't have a theology for leaders.

I hadn't taken a conscious shortcut. I'd just assumed that I and other church leaders behaved in ways that were grounded in the Scriptures we quoted. But when leaders talked heart-to-heart about leadership, I noticed a pattern: we touted our secular sources rather than our religious ones. Now, with alerted ears to hear, I still hear and see that theological blindness in church leaders' practices.

A Better Way

There's a better way for us as religious leaders. Reliable belief-based behaviors can guide our way. We can draw on lasting, dependable, deeper theological foundations to chart our present and future paths forward.

Theology is the distinctive anchor and the obvious guidance system for leaders of faith communities. What if we had three theological threads of a Trinitarian model to guide leaders? What if those master threads grounded leaders in the kingdom of God, the leadership patterns of Jesus, and the work of the Holy Spirit?

Three challenges test leaders every day: time demands, different personalities, and conflicting polarities. Trinitarian beliefs transcend all three of these challenges.

1. **Time threads:** Anchor yourself—past, present, and future—in the kingdom of God. Jesus did. He led kingdomward, a direction that transcends timeframes.

2. **Relational threads:** Treat people the ways modeled and patterned in Jesus' ministry. Cultivate relationships and lead people like Jesus did.

3. **Polarity threads:** Invite the Holy Spirit's power and energy. Venture through open doors with God's Spirit. The Spirit bridges polarities and differences.

The Consultant's Loom

Bob makes a critical point that I often find congregational leaders have overlooked. Before we ever get to our methodology, we must understand our motivating theology. The market is flooded with attractive, compelling, and successful leadership models. Often, clergy and churches are well-versed in concepts carried into the church from the marketplace, but they are relatively ignorant about why God placed them where they are and why their church or faith community is needed in their community.

Clarity around a theological "North Star" came for me in my first pastorate. After six weeks on the job, I realized I was missing something essential to my work. I knew that over time—if I failed to clarify my deeper "why"— I would lose myself in the minutia of ministry. I needed a good answer to why I was pouring my life into ministry.

The quest for that clarity led me on a years-long journey to clarify my sense of mission and theological grounding. Since no one else could do that for me and no book could supply it, I began to dive deep into Scripture, church history, and my personal history to uncover my mission and vision for ministry. What emerged was a God-sized mission that became a compelling and magnetic sense of call. It was genuine to me and my gifts, based upon the life of Jesus, the call of God, and the needs of the world.

I wrote out a personal mission statement 30 years ago that I continue to use and refine. In it I defined the key goals and values of my life and began to think carefully about what life would look like if I lived with intentionality and purpose. Those words and images remain relevant to me, and I think about every opportunity that comes my way through the lens of that larger mission. Without it, I have no doubt I would have lost my way and settled for something far less than what God had envisioned for me.

We hope this book will lead you to do the same. Read, believe, and lead!

Bridging Timeframes
The Father's Kingdom Threads

Time is always a concern for leaders. There's never enough of it. Some unfocused leaders become obsessed with the present moment and their current situation. A religious futurist observes that he often becomes frustrated with pastors. For them, their long-term future is next Sunday—their next sermon and the next gathering of the faithful. We can become so time-bound that we can't ask "what's next." We get stuck in the present.

Effective leaders are time-flexible, operating nimbly in the past, present, and future. We understand the background of our community, can survey the present moment for cues, and are able to look ahead.

The kingdom of God—the strong thread for religious leaders—anchors leaders securely, in part, because it transcends eras of time. God's kingdom, rooted and revealed in history, is unfolding in our present time and will be fully realized in the future. God's kingdom bridges our past, our present, and our future. Simply stated, the kingdom of God transcends timeframes and weaves eras together.

Leading from Kingdom Vision

Time is tough to balance. When leaders think about vision, we too often think exclusively about the future. Consequently, we may disconnect from the past and either largely disregard our history or get frozen in the present. In so doing, we forfeit much of our theological strength. Why? Because the kingdom of God is time-rich and flows across eras. God's kingdom resets our clocks and calendars. The Kingdom opens past and future eons to us. Eternity becomes our timeframe.

When vision is cast for faith communities, God's kingdom transcends and weaves redemptive threads together across eras of time. The Kingdom stewards our healthiest heritage, challenges our current stuck places, and points to God's future for us.

Gregory Jones, formerly at Duke Divinity School and now at Baylor University, claims that clear past identity provides the where and why—by means of "traditioned innovation"[1]—for finding our futures. Jones notes the way Jewish families celebrate Passover. When the family gathers around the meal table, the youngest child asks what makes this day and this gathering different and special. Then the elder narrates the story of this family over time, beginning with the ancient narrative "My father was a wandering Aramean" (Deut. 26:5). The story and the ritual incorporates the family's heritage, its moment in time, and its future. In the same way, leaders hold both tradition and innovation in dynamic tension.

Both history and horizons are woven into our "on purpose" stories. Anchored communities are both old and new, have both identity and creativity, and enjoy both roots and wings. To seize our futures fully, we have to let go of some of the least healthy elements of our pasts. But we still value our heritage and use the best of our best. We tell and interpret our community's healthiest history. We look ahead and reinterpret. We live in the eternal time warp—the then, now, and next—of God's kingdom.

Leaders can only stand where we are in time, but God's kingdom gives us a wrap-around view of time—past, present, and future. Without our pasts we're rootless and have no identity. Without our presents we have no context for our ministry. Without our futures we have no hope. The kingdom of God weaves a godly vision of tomorrow from those past and present threads.

Leading from Kingdom Ideals

"What would Jesus do?" is a decision-guide question we hear asked often and even see on bracelets. In fact, we know exactly what Jesus did. He lived for, taught, modeled, died for, and rose again for the kingdom of God. God's kingdom—the active reign of God in human life—was his "strength thread," his mooring for faith and ministry. Jesus talked about the kingdom of God more than 80 times in the Gospels, more than any other theme. Leaders use our "red letter" New Testaments to remind ourselves constantly that God's kingdom is central. It's right there on the Gospels' pages in red and white, in blood and purity.

The centrality of the kingdom of God in Christian living is beyond dispute. Stanley Grenz expresses it this way: "The kingdom of God is that order of perfect peace, righteousness, justice, and love that God gives to the world. This gift is eschatological, for it comes in an ultimate way only at the renewal of the world consummated in Jesus' return. But, the power of the Kingdom is already at work, for it breaks into the present from the future."[2] The kingdom of God points the way for leaders.

Citizenship in God's kingdom transforms the faithful into "contrast communities." Together, Christians serve up a taste of heaven. We model a countercultural lifestyle in the midst of an unredeemed culture. Kingdom ideals demonstrate sacrificial love in a selfish world and humble service amid the worship of celebrity. Redeemed for distinctive living, the church provides an alternative example of God's highest and best. In response to kingdom ideals, "contrast leaders" embody a timeless and distinctively prophetic edge—the reign of God in and through us.

The kingdom of God sets the highest bar for believers and leaders, providing the foundation for believing and behaving. It's a simple truth. If we want to "be like Jesus" and lead like he did, we'll live out the kingdom of God; we'll bring life and service on earth "as it is in heaven" (Matt. 6:10).

Leading from Kingdom Priorities

Jesus taught consistently on the kingdom of God. In fact, nearly 50 of his parables—his most powerful stories—open with the phrase, "The kingdom of God (or heaven) is like . . ." In our communities of redemption the reign of God, introduced in history, is both a present reality and a future hope. For Christian leaders, God's kingdom is our core belief, our base for behavior, and our time arc.

Jesus' parables, those stories with a purpose, put faces on the gospel. Stories open minds, expand imaginations, and connect people. By personalizing the Kingdom, the parables enlarge our worlds. They also remind us that some unlikely folks become redemptive models and leaders. These leaders' destinies were wed to the kingdom of God.

When Jesus told us to seek God's kingdom first, he was establishing the central anchoring priority for his followers (Matt. 6:33). The Kingdom demonstrates God reigning in and redeeming our lives and our world. The kingdom of God is organic, mystically germinated from "God's seed" rather than "man's deed."[3]

When a seed germinates, its first challenge is to sink a radial root, or taproot, into the host seedbed. Like the heritage of a congregation or ministry community, that taproot provides the center of future life. There will be many branches, leaves, and fruit over the lifespan of the plant, but there will be only one consistent, vital taproot. Healthy churches and their leaders never forget what gardeners know: first roots, then shoots.

In botanical terms, the kingdom of God anchors communities of redemption as their spiritual taproot. For trees and plants, the taproot serves two life-giving purposes. The central taproot stabilizes the tree or plant, holds it upright, and helps it stand strong. And, the taproot sends out secondary roots to gather food and water. The past feeds the future. Like all living things, with stability and nourishment, faith communities can grow.

God's kingdom transforms our yesterdays and todays into tomorrows. For examples, look at the transformations in Jesus' stories and images in Matthew 13. In this pivotal chapter Jesus' teaching moves from the synagogues to the streets, shorelines, and living rooms. And, he uses word pictures—his parables—to transform us:

- Sowers spread seeds on different soils with varied results (vv. 1-9, 18-23): Well-sown and well-received seeds multiply by a hundred-fold. Transformation emerges from receptivity.
- Tiny mustard seeds germinate and grow into impressive trees (vv. 31-32): Small things are transformed into massive growth.
- Yeast permeates and expands loaves (v. 33): The invisible is transformed into the visible.

The kingdom of God awakens our souls and systems, making all things new. Transformation is the work of God's kingdom.

Leading from Kingdom Actions

Our world spins fast. As leaders it's easy to feel overwhelmed and lose track of where we are. When overload causes us to forget who we are, it's called "blurry worry." But God's kingdom is our steady magnetic north—an unerring, orienting navigational guide—for redemptive leaders and communities. True north gives us a place to stand and a direction to face, mooring both directions and destinations for leaders. With our sense of God's calling, we can confidently track and find God's living kingdom.

In the present moment the kingdom of God motivates leaders toward the following actions:

- **Anchoring in the Kingdom first** in all things and arranging other priorities accordingly (Matt. 6:33): The Kingdom reminds us what matters most and guides us in keeping first things first. In the Model Prayer we ask for God's will to be done on earth as in heaven (Matt. 6:10). That's a prayer with a guarantee that it will be heard and answered.

⬜ **Making disciples and loving others** as a basic practice for religious leaders, keeping the Great Commission woven together with the Great Commandment (Matt. 28:16-20, 22:36-40): These two pronouncements are fundamental for religious leaders. We always have a true north orientation, guiding us forward.

⬜ **Living as faithful stewards** of the moment in which God has placed us: It's interesting how often Jesus stopped "as he passed by" to seize the moment for healing, teaching, and transforming lives. He lived in and used his moments.

God's kingdom always has futures and fresh horizons for us. There are new, hope-filled opportunities for our service. Do we see them? Are we ready?

Leading from Kingdom Hope

God's kingdom awakens hope in us and beckons to us to move into the future (Luke 18:5-8, Matt. 22:2-10). The kingdom of God is incarnated in action—first, in the actions of Christ on earth, and, now, in our actions on earth as his proxies and servants. We are called to enact God's reign on earth—to hope and to do God's will on earth "as it is in heaven" (Matt. 6:10).

God, who is mystery, has revealed himself to us bit-by-bit and most vividly in Jesus Christ (Heb. 1:1-3). Those mysteries "sink into" our hearts and slowly appear in our face-to-face faith practices. Some of God's mysteries can be explained in part, but many of them can only be lived out. Jesus' parables, brimming with their mysterious metaphors, intrigued his listeners, causing them to think and explore.

Jesus' rabbinic or teaching role went beyond mere words, however. Jesus knew the limits of his words for leaders, so he enacted parables too. He embodied images, turning teachings into laboratories and demonstrations.

Words and deeds move in tandem, woven into power and beauty. Faith moves from inspiration to perspiration, from principles to practice, from possibilities to realities. As St. Francis of Assisi reportedly instructed us: "Preach the gospel at all times. Use words if necessary."

Happily, Jesus showed us how to lead by example when words have done all they can do. When talk becomes cheap and ineffective, we can enact God's reign of hope in ways that Jesus modeled for us:

☐ **Leading with bread and cup** when shared community needs to be demonstrated (Matt. 26:26-29, Mark 14:22-25, Luke 22:15-20): Vowing not to eat the symbolic meal until the kingdom of God had been fulfilled, Jesus shared the cup and bread at the table with his closest followers. They—and we—then become stewards of the community's gospel message after his death. Gathered around the bread and cup, redemptive community is solemnized and sent into the world.

☐ **Leading with towel and basin** when humble service needs to be modeled (John 13:1): In his last days Jesus showed love for his special followers in an act of humility and service. At supper he rose from the table, took off his coat, wrapped a towel around his waist, took a basin of water, washed his disciples' feet and dried them with the towel. Then he directed them to wash each other's feet. After his betrayer left the dining space, Jesus gave to his faithful friends a new commandment: "Love one another. As I have loved you, so must you love one another. If you have love for one another, then all will know you are my disciples." Simple care for fellow believers is one way leaders demonstrate and make God's kingdom concrete.

☐ **Leading with cheek and shirt** when retaliation becomes too tempt-ing (Matt. 5:38-42): Jesus upended the "an eye for an eye" rule and challenged citizens of God's kingdom to return good for evil; to turn the other cheek and hand over both coat and shirt. Rather than taking revenge, Jesus' followers choose to go the second mile. Aggres-sion is met with love. Kingdom leaders live by higher standards.

☐ **Leading with contrasting actions** when lifestyle differences are the only way to show the way (Matt. 5:43-48): Rather than loving friends and hating enemies, Jesus called for us to love our enemies. Evil is defeated by sacrificial action. Otherwise, we simply reflect the world and forfeit God's perfect way. Later in the Sermon on the Mount, Jesus raised the stakes higher with the Golden Rule: to act toward others in exactly the same manner we want to be treated by them.

☐ **Leading with donkeys and palm fronds** when distinctiveness in leader styles is required (Matt. 21:1-11): Many people expected the

Messiah to seize power in a military coup. But, as foretold by the prophets Isaiah and Zechariah, Jesus entered Jerusalem on a donkey rather than a war horse. Waving palm fronds, the crowds welcomed Jesus with cries of "Praise to David's son! God bless him who comes in the name of the Lord!" As he entered Jerusalem, the people saluted him as "the prophet Jesus, from Nazareth of Galilee."

☐ **Leading from the cliff side** when courage needs to be displayed (Luke 4:16-30): Jesus went back to his hometown of Nazareth and taught in his old familiar synagogue. There he was rejected. Since a prophet has no real local home, Jesus was seen as being "too big for his britches." The synagogue audience took him to the cliff's edge with the intention of throwing him over the brink. There Jesus centered and gathered himself. He walked through the middle of the crowd with a demonstration of great courage.

☐ **Leading around eye logs** when judging others is too easy (Matt. 7:1-6): Jesus challenged his followers to be on their best behavior and to see kindness as a divine expectation. Living better than expected is always a powerful witness.

☐ **Leading with salt and light** when change is needed (Matt. 5:13-14): Salt's purpose is to add flavor to otherwise tasteless food. Light dispels darkness. Salt and light demonstrate God's good works concretely and point to the Kingdom.

Our actions add accent to our words. Strong leaders learn to say and do what's needed. That's a principle Jesus lived out concretely over and over again.

Leading from Kingdom Foundations

Finally, God's kingdom raises the sight-line for our vision, causing us to look upward and outward. When we have eyes to "see" the contours of the Kingdom, we move forward into our futures with confidence. Because of their vision and power, the early Christians "turned the world upside down" (Acts 17:6) and became a capsizing church, a redemptive community that would not settle for the status quo because their leader was a transformer.

God's kingdom isn't "pie in the sky, by and by." When the Kingdom is lived concretely, the hungry eat, the thirsty drink, the stranger finds hospitality, the naked are clothed, the sick are healed, and the prisoner is visited. The practical acts of Christian love reflect God's care for "the least of these" (Matt. 25:31-46). In short, the hopeless discover the gift of God's hope.

Leaders build on the master thread of God's kingdom. It's theologically clear: our faith and practice rest in and on the person and work of Jesus Christ. We leaders base our behaviors on belief in God's Son and his kingdom. He is our model for living and leading. We keep the Kingdom first (Matt. 6:33) and transcend all of time's demands.

The Consultant's Loom

Bob, I think you have named one of our most grievous mistakes as a 21st century church. Far too often I find congregational leaders attempting to reinvent the church without taking seriously their church's past and our history. In the name of relevance, we often neglect the very things that have defined us and made us a distinctive local expression of faith. Granted, simply repeating calendars and programs is no way to create a dynamic future. However, not acknowledging the things that are foundational to the Kingdom that Jesus died to bring to life is a shortcut to irrelevance and decay.

From my experience, vibrant and vital churches and clergy are clear about their past, present, and future.

When it comes to their past they ask questions designed to discover what is right about them. Refusing the temptation to assign blame or cast aspersions on those who have gone before, they instead seek to unearth the qualities and traits that have defined them on their finest day. Using methodologies from the field of appreciative inquiry, there is a dynamic and engaging conversation to be had with any congregation. Approaching our past as a gift to be treasured and analyzed leads one to wonder: "How do we take the best of what was and press it forward?"

Thoughtful congregations further want to be sure that they are living out the vision Jesus taught to his disciples and that the early church used as its blueprint from the outset. No visioning process is complete without a look back: both in terms of the local church and in terms of the people of God. Spending time in Acts 2 and in the writings of the early church is indispensable as we seek to live out that mission in the 21st century. Working through questions about our best traits and actions in the past is a necessary prelude for those who want to build a vibrant future.

In addition to paying attention to our past, vital churches take seriously their present context. The past is our teacher, but it cannot be our master.

One of our most compelling tasks is to listen carefully to our culture and shape the timeless truths of the gospel in such a way that they resonate with our culture.

Following the genius leadership of Paul in making the gospel relevant to multiple cultures and cities, thinking churches study, understand, and appreciate the culture in which they find themselves. Using missionary methodology, they seek to speak is such a way that those in their community comprehend the essence of the gospel. They seek to live and relate in such a way that they are seen as adding to the common good, rather than detracting from it. They seek to find ways to care and minister to people in times of need so that they become an essential part of the fabric of the community. Resisting the urge to chastise, judge, and condemn those around them, they instead live incarnational lives and build relevant churches that are vital cogs in the community around them.

When it comes to the future, vital and vibrant congregations take Bob's ideas about the Kingdom and bring them to life with hope and passion for their community. Having mined their past for their best traits, and taken an honest look at their current setting, they now launch out in bold and provocative ways of living out a dynamic, life-changing faith that is appealing and not repulsive to their community.

Leadership that echoes those three dimensions of time—past, present, future—is most likely to guide a congregation into a vibrant future. Clergy and key leaders must do their own study of their past, present, and future if they are to invite others to do the same. I'm convinced that Paul's sojourn to Arabia before he assumed a leadership role in the early church (Gal. 1:17) was a season of personal reflection by him upon his history, his context, and his emerging call from God. Everyone needs to go to Arabia!

When churches and clergy grasp this grand design that has guided the people of God across the centuries, amazing things become possible.

Notes

[1] L. Gregory Jones, *Faith and Leadership*, "Overcome Mission Drift by Practicing Traditioned Innovation," 17 November 2015, 1-2.

[2] Stanley J. Grenz, *Theology for the Community of God* (Nashville: Broadman and Holman, 1994), 28.

[3] A. M. Hunter, *Introducing New Testament Theology* (London: SCM Press, 1957), 26.

Connecting Personalities
The Son's Relational Threads

A counselor friend once observed: church work would be great, except for the people. But, churches are full of people in the process of redemption. And, religious leadership is people-to-people work. Our ability to relate well to others is a make-or-break success factor for leaders. We are made for community.

Seminaries and ministry training have too often left a "people gap" in training for ministers. We're well trained to work one-to-one in pastoral care and counseling. We're well taught to work one-to-many as we preach and teach.

But, the one-to-a-few skills aren't emphasized as much. That gap can leave a deficit in people skills when we relate to teams, work groups, networks, special interest groups, and cliques. That skills gap also stretches us, because leadership happens largely in a community's one-to-a-few settings.

Inside-Out Leadership

Leaders connect to people, both individually and collectively, to build community. Then we lead our communities from the inside out.

Some leaders are born with great people skills. Other leaders have to work deliberately to master ways of relating to others and creating connections. However we make those connections, relationships become the bridges across which leaders move and work. Great leaders are people smart, using relational intelligence well.[1]

Only occasionally do leaders stand outside their groups and still lead. As exceptions, the Old Testament prophets were insiders who called Israel back to God while standing outside the community. The outside perspective helped them size up the nation's situation clearly and speak with authority. While their lack of connection gave them an outside voice, it left them with no inside leverage. The prophets were heard but not fully heeded. The same happens today.

I learned this inside-outside lesson one cold, blustery winter day. I was marching at the front of a military column, didn't hear a command to halt, and forged ahead. The drill sergeant suddenly appeared at my side. He told me in no uncertain terms to stop marching. I did and stood frozen in place.

With relish, he then predicted my eternal destiny and made some painful observations about my parentage. I glanced back at the column of my fellow trainees. They were laughing and enjoying my predicament way too much. That day I discovered a valuable lesson: Without followers, a leader is just out for a cold walk. Connections are basic for leadership.

Jesus on the Move

It's instructive to watch Jesus connect and lead inside out. The wedding feast at Cana in John 2 was Jesus' first community-wide leadership appearance. Weddings in that culture and era were week-long celebrations of promises, honoring the new bride and groom and treating them like royalty.

The actual movements of Jesus' behaviors at the wedding—from the center to the edge and across the gaps—demonstrate flexible and imaginative leadership. Initially he was in the middle of everything, either as a family friend or perhaps even as a relative. Then he moved to the edge of the party to survey the refreshment situation. Finally, with new wine supplied, he bridged the gaps between sub-groups.

From centers to edges and across gaps, this flexible rhythm maps effective relational leadership. Jesus showed that leadership is more complex than merely "inner circle" versus "outer circle" dynamics.

Each cluster of people in your community's groups offers a special leadership opportunity:

- **Center People:** Successful leaders invest themselves early in that team of core pacesetters who work within the heart of the larger community. In fact, these in-depth relationships are often the first connections a leader cultivates. Center people are the energizers, activists, and tenders of the flame. They ignite the larger community and are keys to the vitality of extended groups.

- **Edge People:** On occasion, leaders move to the edge of their community to see the larger perspective and to look beyond the community for new ministry opportunities looming on the horizon. Interestingly, most religious communities have a few edge people who are "variance sensors." These sensitive souls usually have long experience in the community. This combined perspective of experiences and edges lets variance sensors sense when their communities have wandered off-course and are at variance with their true identity. Their observations can be catalytic calls to begin bringing the larger group back to its core values. Leaders learn to scan the periphery of their communities for former center people who have moved to the edge due to burnout or conflict. These wise persons, now on the edge of the community, may have vision sharpened by time and tension. They are precious resources and guides for leaders.

- **Gap People:** Like Jesus at the Cana feast, leaders learn to oscillate back and forth between centers and edges. Every community needs bridge persons who are sensitive to different elements in their group and who are able to keep sub-groups in conversation with each other. Gap people bridge perspectives and help keep their communities in the "we" mode rather than "us versus them" mindsets. They serve as messengers and runners to make sure communication continues throughout the community.

Mirroring Jesus' Relational Behaviors

As leaders of people, our faith and practice mirror Jesus Christ. Let's look at how Jesus related to four distinct audiences: himself, his co-workers, the crowds who flocked to him, and his persistent critics.

Caring for Self and Soul

Religious leaders grow inside out, cultivating selves and souls. Leaders relate well to themselves before they relate well to others. In the New Testament record we see Jesus crafting himself as a person and leader. Becoming clear about identity and calling are early and continuing challenges for leaders who hope to make a difference in the world.

We know a lot more about Jesus' later ministry than we do about the first 30 years of his life. We read briefly about his birth, trip to Egypt, visit to the temple when he was 12, and a few other references. We know only a few things about the younger Jesus:

- ☐ His family tree shows that he emerged from a diverse multi-generational lineage and from divine action (Matthew 1 and 2).
- ☐ He was born with enemies and had to flee for his life to Egypt (Matt. 2:13-23).
- ☐ He was curious and teachable in the temple and astonished everyone (Luke 2:46-49).

☐ He understood, given the scope of his ministry of redemption, the necessity of teamwork and partnership (Matt. 4:1-11).

☐ He was test-ready and faced his temptations with Scripture's strength and personal clarity (Luke 4:1-13).

☐ He was self-defined and announced "this scripture has been fulfilled in your hearing" (Luke 4:21). Jesus was surrounded on the north, south, east, and west by his relationship with the Father.

☐ He was Scripture-soaked and quoted key passages in his early ministry. For instance, his Nazareth text—the most extensive passage of Scripture Jesus cited—called for care of the poor, captives, and oppressed (Luke 4:14-21).

☐ He practiced "downward mobility," emptied himself, and served the will of God (John 1:10-12, Phil. 2:5-11).

Apprenticing at the knee of Joseph, Jesus learned the woodworkers' art. He learned to create the new, mend the broken, and renew the worn. He discovered how to choose the most beautiful and sturdiest woods. He found the best ways to shape, smooth, and blend components. He understood how to fit and finish projects and people.

But most importantly, while crafting furniture, Jesus crafted his soul. The carpentry shop was likely his incubator for messianic leadership, his studio of the spirit. As Jesus crafted furniture for neighbors, he felt his call crystalizing inside him, clarified his sense of self, and stretched his future. He mulled about the Scriptures that undergirded his faith and heritage. Jesus' "quiet time" and spiritual formation extended for three decades as a child and then a craftsman.

Jesus spent those 30 years in the carpentry shop preparing fully for about 30 months of active and risky ministry. The shop allowed him to discern and clarify his ministry—sifting and sorting and shaping. Jesus grew and matured, readying himself for messianic leadership. Stepping back from the limelight in his early life prepared him to step into the public glare later in life.

Jesus knew who he was and what he stood for. Jesus' self-definition was clear across his lifespan—in the temple at age 12, during the temptations at the launch of his ministry, and in Gethsemane as he faced the cross.

Artisans and craftsmen—like all savvy leaders—hone a sixth sense. They look at futures strategically. Jesus' carpentry craft taught him to look at a tree and envision a table, to see a bit of land and imagine a home. He sharpened his eyes to see the highest potential in people and possibilities.

Leaders grow down and up. The best leaders invest in our own core identity and faith before we step into the spotlight. We mature personally and define who we are in Christ. It's clear that theology is our strength thread.

Mentoring Co-workers

Jesus understood people. He demonstrated again and again how to relate in a timely fashion to a variety of people in all kinds of situations. Jesus invested time and focus in developing his co-workers, especially the small group he lived and worked with for a couple of years.

□ **Jesus approached his co-workers**, called them out, invited them to see and learn firsthand, co-missioned them for ministry, and continued to help them grow in faith and practice. He approached and invited his companions and co-missioners to join him. He "went up into the hills and called to him those whom he desired" (Mark 3:13). Jesus' disciples had a master class in faith development. They watched him first-hand during his public ministry.

□ **Jesus welcomed his co-workers** to spend lots of time with him. He invited them "to be with him" (Mark 3:14) and to "come and see—(and) they stayed with him that day" (John 1:35-41). Transformation happens best when leaders and partners are up close and personal. Jesus' invitation to his disciples "to be with him" points out that he was shaping lifestyles, not just pursuing goals.

□ **Jesus framed his followers' calling** clearly. The Scriptures tell us Jesus sent his followers out "to preach and have authority to cast out demons" (Mark 3:14-15) and to "pray for harvesters" (Luke 10:1-12). He noted "even the demons are subject" to them (Luke 10:17-24) and pointed to their stewardship of power since "whatever you bind (and) loose" had long-term consequences (Matt. 16:13-28).

□ **Jesus spelled out ministry's risks**. He didn't pull any punches. He warned that they will "persecute you" (Matt. 10:16-25), so Jesus' followers were to travel light and to "carry no purse or sandals" (Luke 10:1-12). Evil often confronts leaders. Embodying God's love calls more for childlike innocence than our common adult pursuits of fame and fortune.

Jesus knew that God's kingdom is a community and therefore requires teams of ministers. He called 12 men to ministry (Mark 3:14-15). He instructed and sent out 70 ministers in pairs (Luke 10:1-12). He mentored three—Peter, James, and John—as an inner circle of support and leadership (Matt. 26:36-38). After his death and his resurrection he had 120 believers ready to incarnate the emerging church (Acts 1:15). And, he inspired Paul's pattern of working in missionary teams and of revisiting new faith communities to stabilize and mature them.

The early church used communities of co-workers. For example, the church at Rome built on clusters of leaders. Romans 16:1-16 identified and thanked 24 local leaders, six of them women. Look at the record: Paul introduced and recommended Phoebe for her role in the Roman fellowship. Priscilla and Aquila, a wife and husband who opened their home in Rome to believers, had also worked with Paul in church starts in Corinth and Ephesus. The longer list included freed slaves and even a pair of twin sisters who served behind the scenes in fellowship ministries. Teams of leaders grow sturdy congregations.

Welcoming Curious Crowds

Jesus was a people magnet. His teaching and power drew curious people to him. When crowds gathered around Jesus and followed him, he was moved with compassion, reached out to them, went the second mile for them, and fed them soul and body:

☐ **Jesus read Scripture** with the crowds and identified himself as the fulfillment of its descriptions. In Luke 4:16-30 he shared his Nazareth manifesto, and in John 6:1-40 he called himself "the bread of life."

☐ **Jesus fed souls and bodies** when the crowds gathered. He saw them as "sheep without a shepherd" (Mark 6:30-44) and had "compassion on the crowd" (Mark 8:1-10).

☐ **Jesus made the broken whole**. Among many crowd-based examples of his care and compassion, he healed the man who was deaf (Mark 7:31-37).

As a result of Jesus' words and deeds, crowds of thousands gathered and followed him.

Dealing with Critics

"Contrast" leaders are often criticized and sometimes abused. In the face of those who attacked him, Jesus quoted Scripture, asked thoughtful questions, used object lessons, and calmly stood his ground. And, occasionally, he said nothing at all and simply let silence fill the space.

Expecting lifelong opposition: Jesus experienced opposition from cradle to grave. Herod tried to kill him as an infant. The leaders of his hometown threatened him. His own family thought he was nuts. Religious leaders hounded him. In the end, secular and religious leaders tried him unfairly and executed him, never expecting his resurrection.

Leaders are always at the point, the leading edge, of the community. Consequently, they are often targets of criticism. Jesus found critics in his kinship and faith circles. When family and friends oppose you it's especially painful. When your faith community turns against you or loses trust in you leadership can be crushing. Conflict calls for inner calm, patience with both friend and foe, and the sense that God is present with us. Leaders learn quickly that emotional reactions, while natural, are usually designed for survival and can limit our later options.

Leaders will be resisted. Sometimes opposition is a matter of honest differences. Sometimes conflict comes from human sin and cussedness. So, if you step into the foreground of your community, get ready for opposition. Be ready to define your calling clearly, calmly, and without rancor. Be ready also to hear others' views and to learn gladly from those exchanges. Then, keep the conversation going.

Facing temptations: Jesus' early and most persistent ministry critic was the tempter himself (Matt. 4:1-11, Mark 1:12-15, Luke 4:1-13). Some commentators note that Satan plays with few cards in his hand. He uses the same basic temptations of disordered love over and again. To Jesus he proposed three common shortcuts as Jesus began to change the world. The tempter's logic appealed to key needs:

☐   Pleasure—"You've fasted and searched faithfully for God's will. Now, you deserve to feed your body. Turn stones into bread."

☐   Parade—"You have a brief time to redeem mankind, so let me help you get some attention quickly. Jump off the tower, and I'll get you on the evening news."

☐   Power—"You can use political power to change the world."

Although each "offer" was tempting, Jesus countered with Scripture and resisted all of these short-cuts. Leaders face the same tempting shortcuts. We have to develop an inner radar in order to see shortcuts for what they are and to avoid them.

Modeling behavior: In the midst of his critics, Jesus defined himself with caring and curing. His actions of restoring health and wholeness sharply contrasted "the rule of God" with the religious rule-keeping demanded by the Pharisees. Among other miracles, he healed the paralyzed man who had been lowered through the roof (Luke 5:17-26) and gave sight to the blind man (John 9:1-41). With Jesus, human need trumped religious guidelines (Luke 6:1-11). He demonstrated a better way.

Reacting gently: Jesus drew sharp contrasts with his critics without inciting intentional confrontation. Remember how he pointed to the differences between the attitudes and behaviors of his Pharisee host and the sinner who bathed his feet (Luke 7:36-50)? Leaders know that a demonstration of love is generally the best argument for changing lives and behaviors.

Relying on Scripture: Jesus indicted burdensome, blinding religion with Scripture's clear differences and declared "woes" (Matthew 23). When faith becomes negative or evil, religious leaders stand our ground and name the offending patterns.

Showing calm demeanor: Jesus faced the religious experts calmly. The religious hierarchy felt threatened by him. His teaching and his responses to their questions left the Pharisees and the Jews without theological footing.

Some critics simply don't like you. They don't want to talk with you. In that case, there's probably no way to relate or to win them back. They will assume they are mistake-free, or assume you're inferior and flawed beyond help, or not mind if you suffer, or make the situation about them.

Staying committed: At his trial Jesus stood up to evil, never giving in or giving up (Luke 23:1-5). His calling and our redemption were more crucial to him than his own life.

In the Gospels we see how Jesus behaved as he led. He developed his core self and soul within the kingdom of God. He gave us clear examples of how to lead well with an array of audiences, his co-workers, the crowds, and his critics. In each case his modeling gives leaders a template for how to lead people more effectively.

The Consultant's Loom

Bob, you have named the primary challenge most leaders fail to navigate: self-reflection. The ability to conduct a fearless internal inventory is at the heart of great leadership. Jesus obviously spent vast amounts of time and effort understanding his call and motivation as Messiah. His proactive efforts to pull away and prepare himself by feeding his soul are a model and inspiration to any thoughtful leader.

Reading his story in the Gospels, it appears this preparation meant that he was seldom surprised by either failure or success, and he remained less anxious than those around him because of this clarity of mission and vision.

Most of us resist such thoughtful reflection upon our motives, hidden agendas, and covert dreams. The depth of honesty that requires makes us uncomfortable and anxious. We often see ourselves in the negative examples of leadership that surround us and resist peering into the parts of us that we know need work. We, like David, end up doing things and becoming someone we never imagined we would or could become.

What if we, instead, followed the lead of Jesus and practiced healthy leadership basics? The humility and transparency you describe is at the heart of any effective leader. Jesus' work with individuals, small groups, and large groups resonates with ministers who spend every week in the same circles.

The ministers and lay leaders I encounter who are highly effective have spent time preparing themselves for their "Queen Esther Moment" (Est. 4:14). They have a sense of being placed in a situation "for such a time as this" by both seen and unseen forces. Their prevailing spirit is that of humility at being used by God for such significant tasks.

They also realize that the example of Moses being urged by Jethro to invite others into the leadership circle in order to enhance his effectiveness is essential to any healthy leadership model (Exod. 18:18). Encouraging and raising up new leaders is at the heart of a great leader's work. Taking to heart Paul's command to "outdo one another in showing honor" (Rom. 12:10), they create a culture of encouragement and affirmation.

Effective ministers and lay leaders acknowledge that no one of us can do our work alone. We all need to be part of a leadership community and culture. The metaphor of the human body being the organizing image of the church (1 Corinthians 12) is not lost on them.

Godly leaders find those who are truth tellers and invite them to hold the leader accountable. All great leaders need a Nathan to speak truth to their power (2 Sam. 12:7). Such conversations can help keep us from the illusion of perfection and the resulting conflicts.

One of the best gifts God has given me along the way has been a series of women and men who would tell me the truth about myself. Many days the conversations were hard and bracing. Early in my ministry I found myself resenting and resisting such conversations. I avoided them or dismissed them as coming from unreasonable critics who didn't know the whole story.

Gradually I came to understand that these people were not a curse upon my life, but rather a gift. Early in my ministry I faced a congregational situation that seemed hopeless and demoralizing.

After one especially frustrating meeting a wise gentleman simply asked me: "Do you want to know what went wrong in there?"

I replied: "Sure I do! No one seemed to understand what I was saying!"

"Actually, you stopped listening and started pushing your agenda five minutes into the meeting. You lost everyone, and you never knew it."

In a flash I realized how right he was. My absorption with my plans had made me blind to everyone and everything else in the room. Our next meeting began with a humble and heart-felt apology from me, and the tone and tenor of the project changed that day, and we ended up doing some amazing things together—all because my Nathan spoke the truth to me.

As hard and humbling as it was to hear those words, the feeling of having someone speak the truth in love was exhilarating. I began to invite people to talk *to* me and not *about* me. I worked hard (and still do) to hear their words in as non-defensive a manner as possible. The result has been fresh eyes and senses for recognizing God's spirit and the needs and dreams of those around me. It is a constant challenge, but it's one that promises depth and meaning never found without thoughtful reflection.

Most of us have learned the hard way that we need inner strength and a core resolve that is anchored in something more solid than the inevitable critiques or the applause of the moment. Ministry is seductive in that it lures us to believe either the very best or the very worst about ourselves. An internal compass guided by the Holy Spirit and a set of expectations and an agenda that transcends the present is indispensable in that struggle.

In our consulting work with congregations and faith communities, the greatest joy we experience is when a local church and its leadership grasp these essentials and collectively operate out of a humble sense of divine calling to a Kingdom agenda. To do so means focusing our attention first on *why* we exist in this time and place. Before we ever move to *what* we will do and *how* we will do it, we must wrestle mightily with our *why* in the providence of God's kingdom. Clarifying answers then give us the ability to envision a future that exceeds what we could ever do out of our own strength. When that happens, God-sized dreams really do come true.

Note

[1] Daniel Goleman, Richard Boyatzis, and Annie McKee, *Primal Intelligence: Realizing the Power of Emotional Intelligence* (Boston: Harvard Business School, 2002).

Transcending Polarities
The Spirit's Power Threads

Today's leaders face a fractured world. Contention, competition, fear, and disagreement tear us apart. From every quarter we hear "us" versus "them." "No" drowns out "yes." There are polarities everywhere. Our world is basically defined by differences, battles, paradoxes, contradictions, and conflicts. It's no wonder the family tree of my Baptist faith has more than four dozen branches in the United States alone.

Polarities introduce paradoxes. Today is a tough time to lead, but it's also a great moment to be a leader. There are both challenges and possibilities everywhere.

Look down the street, and you hear your angry neighbor fussing with someone. Go to your family's reunion, and there's your crazy cousin again. In some quarters the Civil War's still being fought. "From here's" don't trust "come here's." Millennials are at odds with Baby Boomers. Perfectly reasonable folks nearly come to blows over their favorite sports teams. And, Westboro Baptist Church pickets everyone. These opposing polarities define our era and our opportunities even more sharply.

So, how do we bridge oppositions? Amid polarities leaders stay alert for opportunities for positive ministries, looking for new doors on the horizon. Acts is a case study in how the Holy Spirit raised up leaders to overcome chasms and stalemates; those leaders then took risks for expanded futures. Possibilities emerged in every chapter of Acts. As the fledgling church faced barrier after barrier, God's Spirit opened door after door. Leaders followed the Spirit and kept the early church on the move.

God's Spirit, Our Futures

The book of Acts begins (1:3) and ends (28:31) with conversations about leaders' primary theological thread: the kingdom of God. The 30-year sweep of Acts, when the church expanded like a prairie fire from Jerusalem across the known world, was propelled by the Spirit of God. The kingdom of God was on the march.[1] The Good News unfolded seamlessly from polarities to possibility after possibility in Acts.

Jesus described the Holy Spirit variously as our comforter, advocate, and paraclete. When Scripture assures us that we will never be abandoned or orphaned, it's reminding us that God's Spirit is always alive and lively in our lives. The Holy Spirit is our constant companion, our keen observer, our supportive encourager, our fair evaluator, our persistent pest, and our doorman to futures. The Spirit is with us—in times of need, in seasons of disobedience, in moments of despair, and before open doors of opportunity. God's Spirit accompanies us always.

Luke's second volume is formally called the Acts of the Apostles, named for the leaders of the early church's vanguard. But the book more accurately records the redemptive acts of the Holy Spirit. It's the Spirit's work that forms the dynamic thread of breakthroughs shared throughout this exciting book.

Remember that God's Spirit is in us, with us, and ahead of us now. God continues to transform us and our world. As leaders with God's Spirit setting the pace, faith flows future-ward and helps us clear polarity's hurdles.

Bridges and Ditches

The Holy Spirit guided the early church across the polarities of "bridges and ditches."[2] Some historic factors, or bridges, favored the missionary advance of the church. On the other hand, some matters hindered the spread of the gospel and became barriers, or ditches. Major cultural bridges included:

☐ **Roman peace:** The Roman Empire's peace, spanning roughly from the Danube and Rhine rivers to the basin of the Euphrates, created stability and a network of roads. With easy travel, no need for visas, and safety on the roads, missionaries moved freely.

☐ **Greek language:** Greece may have been conquered politically by the Romans, but Greek language and culture captured Roman tongues and minds. While Latin was the official language of the empire, Greek became the conversational language. In Greek, Paul was able to address Roman officials and the centurion (Acts 21:37ff). This common language, spoken across the Roman Empire, opened doors for the New Testament and made evangelization easier.

☐ **Jewish faith:** The Romans may not have understood the Jews in the empire, but the religious practices of the Jews were generally respected and left alone. When the Old Testament was translated into Greek, Roman citizens learned more about the Jews' mono-theism, history, and practices. A measure of comfort with Judaism, in turn, facilitated toleration and acceptance of Christianity.

In contrast, historic and cultural barriers, or ditches, made missionary work more difficult. Those ditches included some significant challenges for the early church:

- ☐ The Jews didn't understand leaders without formal credentials.
- ☐ The Jews couldn't accept a messiah on a cross.
- ☐ The Jews didn't see how people not of Abraham's seed could belong to religious communities.
- ☐ The Romans didn't want their state religion undercut.
- ☐ The Romans couldn't tolerate secret societies.
- ☐ The Romans didn't appreciate the Christian's family ethic.
- ☐ The Romans couldn't celebrate a crucified carpenter.

To change the Roman Empire in the span of a single generation, leaders of the early church became stewards of both bridges and ditches. They moved across the bridges gladly and waded through the ditches carefully. They wove blessings and barriers together.

Divides—Persisting and Challenging

It's no surprise that creeds and cultures and continents clashed as the early church expanded. They still do. But God's Spirit transcends creedal, cultural, and continental polarities. These differences can still be overcome with leadership.

Leaders in Acts relied on the Holy Spirit's power. One of Luke's favorite descriptions of the Spirit's work is "unhindered." In fact, 30 percent of the New Testament references to this word about victorious freedom in Christ appear in Acts (as illustrated in 8:31, 10:47, 28:31). Unhindered preaching of the kingdom of God is literally the last word in Acts (28:31). The unfinished work of the gospel has become our stewardship as leaders.

Just as we've earlier anchored a theology for leaders in God's kingdom and in Jesus' relational patterns, let's now read Acts with an eye for how the Holy Spirit empowers us as leaders. In the Holy Spirit polarities are bridged, horizons are made accessible, and new ministry possibilities are seized.

Transcending Religious Polarities

Religious differences have always united and divided America, and they still do. The New World attracted religious expressions that the Old World resisted. Here in America we discovered again a consistent and enduring pattern. Our faith brings and holds our faith communities together—until our faith creates a contrast or a competition with someone else's faith. Then, we fight over our beliefs and biases.

Religious warfare in the first century shows up over and over again in Acts. Jews and Gentiles, synagogues and churches, ethical faiths and pagan practices, Christians and traditional religion: they find themselves at odds. And repeatedly, God's Spirit changes hearts and resolves differences. Religious polarities become possibilities for the Spirit to weave new faith tapestries.

Early and often Acts speaks candidly about clashes of creeds. Persecution of Christians began in the early church when the Sadducees took offense at the disciples for assuming a rabbinic teaching role about Jesus' resurrection (4:1-31). Later in Acts the Pharisees, the Herodians, and a variety of pagan groups—each with their own reasons—expanded the persecution of the People of the Way. Religion divided faiths.

Local Versus World Views

Look at the story of Stephen, the first Christian martyr. Local versus world religion clashed in Acts 6 and 7. Stephen's teaching and the miracles he performed placed him in "dispute" with local powers. Stephen's wisdom and the power of the Spirit were too much for traditional forces to resist, so they fought dirty—a practice still seen in church conflicts. They accused him of blasphemy against Moses and God as well as against the holy place and the law. They arranged for false witnesses to testify before the high priest.

When asked to answer the charges against him, Stephen simply reviewed Hebrew history. He pointed out that God had never limited himself to any one "holy" nation. And, with candor, he noted that the movable tabernacle was a better fit for God's universal work of redemption than Jerusalem's local temple. And, worse yet for them, he pointed out that they, his accusers, had violated the law they were now accusing Stephen of breaking.

The crowd's explosive reaction was immediate. They "ground their teeth" and angrily called for death by stoning. Whether a lynch mob or an official execution, the result was the same. Stephen was killed while asking God that this sin not be held against his accusers.

How was this polarity transformed by the Spirit? It took a while. Saul had "consented" to Stephen's death. Saul's zealotry became mainstream in an intense regional wave of persecution against the church that followed Stephen's stoning. He ravaged the church like a wild animal, dragging families from their homes and throwing them into prisons (Acts 8:1-3). Saul would have to become converted to Christ and renamed Paul before he stopped his leadership of widespread mistreatment against Christians, but the Spirit was at work.

Believing—or Not

Next we come to the Damascus Road. Saul, still breathing fire, was authorized to clear the religious debris of the Way from the synagogues in Damascus. He planned to bring the Christian heretics, both men and women, back to Jerusalem in chains.

Then, all of Saul's beliefs and background were placed in the crosshairs. Jesus confronted him in a flash of light and asked him pointblank why he was persecuting Christians. In the spotlight the persecutor chose to reverse his life course and to become one of the persecuted Christians. It was a blinding, disorienting decision that threw him into internal disarray. In Damascus and then in Arabia (Gal. 1:17), Saul began a discerning season of sifting and sorting, of soul-rehab and self-discovery.

Saul, soon to be renamed Paul, had timely help in his transition. The Spirit gave him guides for every step in his new journey. First, Ananias met Paul in Damascus with the restoration of sight, the anointing of the Holy Spirit, and food at the table of fellowship (Acts 9:17-19). Fellow believers there, after initial skepticism, accepted Paul and saved him from a murderous plot by lowering him over the city wall to safety.

Upon returning to Jerusalem later (Acts 9:26-30), the disciples were also afraid of Paul and his well-deserved reputation at first. But Barnabas, his mentor-to-be, vouched for him. (Interestingly, the Greek word for Barnabas is a cognate of "paraclete," meaning "called alongside." The encouragement Barnabas gave Paul is a reminder of the emotional support leaders need as we grow and serve. When faith is stirred, a guide or mentor is needed to help us find our new way.) Although Jerusalem's believers accepted Paul, the Hellenists set out to kill him. Mercifully, the brethren spirited him out of town safely.

Paul personified how the Holy Spirit moved the early church ahead. He took part in all three phases of expansion in Acts. He was there during the Jewish years in Jerusalem as the church began to emerge. In those days the Hebrew leaders were in charge and Christians were part of Jewish life (Acts 1:6–6:7).

Then Stephen, Philip, and unnamed men from Cyprus and Cyrene stepped into the foreground of the movement (Acts 6:8–12:25). These new leaders thought and acted globally. They reached into the Greek world effectively.

Finally, the focus of the faith moved beyond Palestine and the synagogues to reach pagans directly (Acts 13–28). Paul's missionary journeys and his leadership were the primary features of this stage of outreach.

Paul's new beliefs and identity set him on the road to defining the faith and practices of the early church. His letters to the churches show his transformation from creedal cop to church starter across the empire.

Freedom from the "Greater Burden"

The Jerusalem Council in Acts 15 marks a watershed in first-century religion. In the early Christian movement Gentiles had to be circumcised in order to belong to the new community. In this tradition Moses had to be obeyed before Jesus could be followed. This approach created first- and second-class Christians in some quarters. Some Pharisees strongly insisted that without circumcision there was no salvation.

Paul and Barnabas debated these traditional Pharisees. Finally, an appeal was made to the apostles and elders in Jerusalem to settle the difference.[3] In the gathering Peter spoke about the gift of the Holy Spirit to all and appealed to the council to remove any yokes that minimized God's universal grace. Then Paul and Barnabas described how God's Spirit had worked among the Gentiles, giving evidence to support Peter's appeal. James, perhaps the most influential of the Jerusalem leaders, agreed that circumcision wasn't required for salvation, but he asked for Gentile believers to respect Jewish practices.

A letter went to churches and regions where the guardians of the past had created tension. The testimony of the Jerusalem Council was clear: "God, who knows men's hearts, bore his own witness to them by them the Holy Spirit just as he had done to us too . . . our beloved Barnabas and Paul, men who have risked their lives for the sake of our Lord Jesus Christ (and) it was the decision of the Holy Spirit and of us to lay upon you *no greater burden* than these necessary things" (Acts 15:8, 28).

Being a faithful believer and leader was and is challenging enough without extra burdens. In terms of the circumcision issue, the polarity was closed for Christians and peace was restored in the emerging churches.

Transcending Cultural Polarities

Cultural divides are obvious in Acts and perhaps more clearly seen and reported by Luke, the New Testament's only non-Jewish writer. Cultural differences divide us today too. In some circles America's melting pot has been heated to a boil. Non-English languages, distinctive traditions and customs, different nations of origin, and new lifestyles: all continue to create a variety of polarities and barriers to faith's acceptance.

Will Herberg's classic sociological description of our nation's triple melting pot, Protestant-Catholic-Jew,[4] has traced the ways immigration and acculturation shaped religious life in the United States over the last century or so. Those cultural differences persist and challenge leaders to this day. And, as more religions and faith expressions have arrived on our shores, the polarities have continued to multiply.

When Languages Collide

The Jerusalem church included different language groups. "Murmuring" in the church arose over what was perceived as neglect of the Greek-speaking widows and favoring of the Aramaic-speaking widows (Acts 6:1-8). The 12 apostles, placed in a triangle between opposing views,[5] called a town meeting and asked for leaders to be selected to bridge this breach.

One way to face polarities is to get opposing parties to talk with and listen to each other. The apostles' action brought the two sides of the disagreement together to explore and resolve the issue. As a result, seven new leaders were chosen and empowered to assure equal care for those in need.

Two of these leaders, Stephen and Philip, had ministries beyond this early division. The Spirit had more work for them to do.

Reaching Out to Non-believing Groups

Paul's second missionary journey made multiple cultural leaps forward. Money, idolatry, and magic were faced squarely. New converts came from a range of religious perspectives.

In Philippi (Acts 16:11-34), Paul and Silas crossed the commercial class. They healed a slave girl, angering her owners by taking away their source of income. Paul and Silas were beaten and thrown into prison where the Philippian jailer was converted after their midnight songfest (vv. 25-34). This is the first instance of a Gentile with no Jewish background being converted out of paganism. The gospel had reached Acts' final target group.

In Athens (Acts 17:16-34), Paul went into the marketplace to debate with Greek philosophers about their many idols. They were addictively curious about Paul's teaching of a new philosophy about Jesus. His sermon about an unknown god caused some to mock and others to believe. The gospel moved forward again. Believers from a different source were evangelized.

In Corinth (Acts 18:1-11), Paul found fellow tentmakers and believers. Together they appealed for faith in the synagogue. There, Crispus, the ruler of the synagogue, converted to Christianity and was baptized with his entire household. The Spirit opened so many spiritual doors in Corinth that Paul stayed and ministered there for a year and a half.

In Ephesus (Acts 19:8-20), Paul took a huge step forward. A Hebrew of the Hebrews broke with the synagogue. He had preached the kingdom of God to them, but they called the Way evil. So, Paul left the synagogue with a group of new believers and stayed in Ephesus with them for two years. Some spiritualists competed with Paul for a time and then, in the face of miracles, left their magic materials behind and followed Christ.

God's Spirit transcends cultures. The pattern seen in the early church continues today.

Transcending Global Polarities

Acts traces Christianity's spectacular arc from Jerusalem to unexpected places where the new faith took root. Our faith's roots in the Middle East soon reached into Africa, Europe, and beyond, as the New Testament and early church history record. Evangelizing across civilizations and continents was common in the early church. That success created a new set of polarizing challenges.

Our world thinks and acts globally. A troubling event on the other side of the globe reverberates around the world and shakes our streets too. Some religious and political chasms seem too wide to cross. America is confused when missionaries appear on our shores and contrast themselves with what we've taken for granted. Then, God's Spirit shows us the way to bridge massive differences.

From the beginning of the Acts' narrative, the wider world was targeted for evangelization. Christians were sent beyond Jerusalem to Judea, Samaria, and to the end of the earth (1:8). Traditional religious groups resisted Christianity's momentum to move outward. Consequently, the gospel moved beyond local synagogues to plant global churches. New believers were on the move. The Holy Spirit was far ahead of them, blazing the way forward.

In the face of early persecution, believers were scattered by the Spirit in a variety of new places. By the time of Stephen's death, the gospel had already been preached in Jerusalem. Then, outreach extended to the Samaritans.

Additionally, Gentiles, who were students of Judaism but weren't proselytes yet, heard the Good News. Finally, pagans such as the Philippian jailer heard and accepted the gospel. Christianity was on the move toward new peoples and places.

Philip went to Samaria in Acts 8, where he preached and healed the lame and paralyzed. In cultural terms, a Greek Christian evangelized the inter-married Samaritans. Joy resulted. In global terms, the ends of the world were just over the horizon.

Then God dispatched Philip to a road leading to Gaza. There he met an Ethiopian eunuch, a government official in this African nation. The Ethiopian was reading from Isaiah. Likely, the eunuch was a "God-fearer" and an admirer of monotheism's high ethical standards. He probably wasn't a proselyte since the Jews considered him to be mutilated. Philip was eager to preach, and the eunuch was ready to believe. The new convert asked to be baptized, and his request was immediately granted. The gospel was welcomed across national, racial, and religious polarities.

Paul wanted to go east but couldn't, so the Holy Spirit invited him to move west. The Macedonian call (Acts 16:6-10) helped the early church look beyond the Roman Empire's territories in the Middle East, Africa, and some sections of Europe. The "ends of the earth" raised leaders' horizons high. When life gets complicated, leaders focus on the most productive direction.

Moving from Polarities to Horizons

Leadership is a two-sided coin. Communities need leaders, or they risk becoming sheep without shepherds. Leaders need communities, or they risk talking only to themselves. God's Spirit opened the pages of Acts with the creation of a new, redeeming community. We shouldn't be surprised. Redemption is the work of the Spirit of God.

The geographic, ethnic, and cultural futures of the early church are mapped in one verse: Jerusalem, Judea, Samaria, and the rest of the world (Acts 1:8). God's kingdom was on the move. Agile leaders were being called and prepared for each new step in the redemptive journey.[6]

At the end of Acts the Kingdom remained central and found leaders "preaching the Kingdom of God and teaching about the Lord Jesus Christ quite openly and unhindered" (28:25). Acts records only the opening chapter of the expansion of futures in the early church. With faithful leaders, God's kingdom is always on the march.

Leaders need a longer and larger view of calling for their communities and for themselves. The Holy Spirit stretched the perspective of Acts' leaders—from local to regional to global, from Jews to Gentiles to a wide world of ethnicities and backgrounds. Our ministry horizons will expand when enlightened by God's Spirit as the guide for conflict resolution and peacemaking. In spite of polarities, a new redemptive tapestry will be woven by the Spirit.

Religious leadership is a calling for us, a quest to discover and to embody the nature of a mysterious God. Faithful leaders stand on a theological foundation. When beliefs anchor us as leaders, our behavioral options are clarified and can be built on with confidence. Theology is the "strength thread" for church leaders. It's that simple. And, it's that challenging.

The Consultant's Loom

We often forget that we stand on the shoulders of church leaders who have met and conquered challenges equally as daunting as ours. Healthy leaders are always reconnecting to the core strengths of their faith community that have been revealed over time. From those stories we discover what is "right" about us, and we seek to push those traits into the future with imagination and passion.

I served as pastor of a church that faced significant facility and financial challenges. As we began to pray and dream about our daunting future, we also began to discover our remarkable history. It turns out that our church had been used as a Union hospital during the Civil War. The damage inflicted upon the building was so massive that it was torn down immediately following the war.

The post-war years were hard, lean years in the community. Raising money to rebuild the church building took a back seat to simple survival. Gradually, the people pulled together enough resources to dig a foundation and a basement for a future church. That was all they could afford. For nearly a decade they met in a dark, windowless basement for worship. Finally, a key leader decided that the time had come to sacrifice and build a proper facility. He personally gave money and labored generously, inspiring others to match his commitment. Within a short time a magnificent sanctuary emerged for use by the congregation for decades to come.

When we told that story of our forefathers and mothers, we were reminded that our 21st century challenges are rather tame compared to the ones previous generations faced. We were inspired toward a sacrificial attitude that resulted in another remarkable display of faith and stewardship on our watch.

Bob reminds us that our cultural challenges and perplexing polarities are nothing new to God's people. The book of Acts is a manual for how God's people are to live in, but not be seduced by, their world. The polarities and challenges that confronted the early church remain our challenges.

On a regular basis I find churches attempting to employ either/or solutions to both/and problems. Doing so always produces high anxiety, frustration, and conflict. Roy Oswald has taught us to recognize that many of our modern challenges require us to negotiate a continuum of possibilities rather than seek a final, declarative solution.[7]

We cannot give ourselves, for example, fully to an internally or externally focused church, because neither model is sufficient by itself to bring the Kingdom to bear upon our culture. We cannot live exclusively in the world of either tradition or innovation, for one without the other leaves us in arrears with sizable portions of our culture. We cannot depend exclusively upon either laity or clergy leadership to guide us well. Both need one another to create the kind of congregation Christ envisions for today.

Leadership in that tension is mature, thoughtful, and deeply grounded in biblical and church history. It has a theological underpinning that enables us to trust the Holy Spirit to use our best efforts in ways we cannot fully comprehend. Our leadership must employ an adaptive strategy if we are to manage the waves of change and challenges coming our way. Doing so means living in the tension between innovation and tradition and becoming comfortable with those stressors. Guiding a congregation toward that same Spirit is a gradual and challenging task. It is not to be done overnight or by using simplistic methods, but by being present in community over time.

Leaders of vibrant churches learn to employ the same mindset that the early church modeled for us: God's people, organized around a Christ-centered mission, seeking to be and make disciples in a world that misunderstands us. While our challenges are substantial, we must also believe that there has never been a better time to be God's people on a mission of hope, help, and healing for our world.

Bob, what you are describing in this chapter is the world we live in. What we seek to find is that theological center that enables us not only to survive but also to thrive in the 21st century.

Notes

[1] Michael Green, *Thirty Years That Changed the World: The Book of Acts for Today* (Grand Rapids: Eerdmans, 2002).

[2] Ibid., 11-24.

[3] Roger Martin, *The Opposable Mind: How Successful Leaders Win Through Integrative Thinking* (Boston: Harvard Business School, 2007).

[4] Will Herberg, *Protestant-Catholic-Jew: An Essay in American Religious Sociology* (Garden City, NY: Doubleday, 1955).

[5] Peter L. Steinke, *How Your Church Family Works: Understanding Congregations as Emotional Systems* (Herndon, VA: Alban Institute, 2006), 45-60.

[6] Robert D. Dale, *Growing Agile Leaders: Coaching Leaders to Move with Sure-Footedness in a Seismic World* (Hickory, NC: Coach Approach Ministries, 2011).

[7] Roy Oswald and Barry Johnson, *Managing Polarities: Eight Keys for Thriving Faith Communities* (Herndon, VA: Alban Institute, 2009).

PART 2

Weaving Leader Maturity
Leading from Threads of Growing Wisdom

Welcome to a second set of threads for our leadership tapestry: the process of cultivating psychological maturity. Let's weave these wisdom threads together. Let's grow up and grow into our leadership opportunities.

Here's the brutal truth: maturity has a beginning but no end. As long as we draw breath, we have a chance to "grow up." Paul calls this maturation quest "the fullness of Christ" (Eph. 4:13).

Let's explore our maturity pilgrimage. As we look at the learning challenges for each life stage and the implication of each stage for leaders' stories, ask yourself:

☐   What maturity challenges have I already faced well?
☐   What maturity challenges are still unfinished for me?
☐   How can I "grow up"?

"Launch" Threads

Leader Maturity for Teens and 20s

Weaving foundations for younger leaders begins early—when we "launch." Launching a life and enriching faith aren't individual or independent processes. Younger leaders depend a lot on others' help and blessing. Young leaders bloom and grow on grace, on being praised for our efforts, on enough space to accept the benefit of the doubt given to novices, and on the encouragement and guidance of our elders as we cultivate self and soul.[1]

The journey toward maturity for young leaders during our teens and young adulthood includes basic questions and generous gifts. We are just launching our leadership pilgrimage. The process is lively.

Leader Incubators

"When did others first see you as a leader?" That question kicked off the first session of the first level of Virginia Baptists' Young Leaders' Program from 1989 to 2009, the 20 years of its duration.[2] What was the most common answer from these emerging leaders? "During my early teens." They had started early with the encouragement of others.

When asked "where were you when you first realized that others saw leader strengths in you that you hadn't seen in yourself yet," two common answers commonly emerged: "My church's youth group" or "At my school," especially in music and sports. A scattered few mentioned service groups, such as Scouts or 4-H. Those young leaders who had stepped to the front of their peers both at church and at school had received a booster shot of leadership along with confirmation from varied groups and in different settings.

Interestingly, smaller churches and schools provided the best leader incubators for these young leaders. These compact settings allowed potential to be spotted in early adolescence. More importantly, these more intimate groupings offered expanded early opportunities to step out front and try on leadership roles with lower risks.

When asked "who guided you as a new leader," most of these young leaders could name a mentor instantly. Their lists of guides and encouragers often included teachers, coaches, or pastors. Someone had recognized teen talent and had then nurtured these novice leaders. What about you?

☐   When did you become a leader?

☐   In what settings did you discover your leadership gifts?

☐   Who opened leadership doors for you and guided you?

☐   How are you paying those early encouragements forward?

☐   Who's looking to you for blessing and opportunity?

☐   How can you keep your personal faith lively and vital for this younger stage of life?

Mapping the Teen Leader Journey

Psychologists note that teenagers face two foundational questions about identity and direction in life: Who am I becoming, and what will I do with my life?[3]

Who am I becoming?

The search for self and soul are intensely personal quests, customized on the run. Life isn't a fully marked road. We have to find our way toward maturity. We begin to tell our own story as teens, and our stories begin to explain us then as well.

As a teen, my life and faith began to unfold in two directions simultaneously: successes and failures, opportunities and limits. Both forces shaped self and soul in me and left a lifelong imprint on me as a leader.

Birth order and family dynamics. On the positive side, birth order is a shaper of selves and souls. As my family's firstborn, I was a blessed child. I was trusted with early responsibilities.

My family moved to a new farm in 1950. Actually, it was our old farm, bought by my parents in 1938. But World War II caused a need for an Army training camp in the Ozark Mountains of southwestern Missouri, and the federal government bought a huge tract of land, including our farm. In 1950 the land was put up for resale, and original owners were given the first right of refusal. Most families could no longer subsist on the "40 acres and a mule" lifestyle of Depression days, so they didn't buy back. My parents, however, bought our original 160 acres and then more than doubled our land holdings, with about 40 acres in the river bottom and more than 300 acres of pasture in the mountains.

My dad served as a prison guard during our early years back on the farm. Being a tower guard was intense duty, and, to complicate his life even more, his schedule rotated to a new work shift every 28 days. So, Dad was not available for many farm chores. By my earliest teen years I was driving our tractor in the fields, milking our cows, and putting up hay. It was hard work for a teen, but I learned to take charge and be responsible for tasks. In many ways I grew up in a leader laboratory.

I was being shaped by a frontier mentality.[4] Like any new frontier, when my family reestablished our farm, we cleared fields, built new barns, and started from scratch. It was natural. My grandfathers had worked together on a cattle ranch in Oklahoma while it was still Indian territory. My maternal grandfather homesteaded in western Kansas. The American frontier was in my blood.

My early leader lab extended beyond our family farm. I was my high school's top student, president of the student body, and a three-sport athlete. During the already-busy summers I played in a semi-pro baseball league too. Additionally my parents had me in church every time the doors opened. After spending my teens as a religious seeker, I professed faith the summer before I left for college and became involved in my church at a new level. When I began college I "majored" in Air Force ROTC and rose quickly through the ranks. As you can see, while a teen I had lots of practice arenas for leadership.

Life's crucibles. On the negative side I faced several tough tests or "crucibles," especially as a college freshman. I had finished high school with a clear life plan. I was engaged to my high school girlfriend, had a full scholarship to the University of Missouri's engineering school, and intended to fly Air Force jets. One, two, three . . . all precisely planned, all clearly in focus. I thought I was 10 feet tall and bullet-proof. Then, during my first semester of college, all three of my life goals evaporated within weeks. I walked in on my girlfriend's wedding to another guy. I found I didn't have the math background for engineering. I discovered my eyesight wasn't keen enough to pilot fast planes. Strike one, strike two, strike three . . . I was out.

I struggled for a while. Then I decided I might be down, but I wasn't out. I got up, dusted myself off, and went back to basics. The second semester of my freshman year became a time of profound discovery. First, I had to find ways to grow up fast by absorbing the tough lessons failure forced on me. During those difficult months I identified two courses that fascinated me: psychology and writing. Psychology became a way to understand myself and others, and writing provided ways to clarify and communicate my ideas. Those grounding interests pointed to some life and career options for me.

When I re-dug my foundations, my spiritual life deepened too. For the first time in my life I chose my own church rather than go to my family's church. As it turned out, my church was across town from my dorm. So I walked several miles to church each weekend. One Sunday a friend asked to go to church with me. As we walked and walked he finally laughed and said, "You don't go to church. You go on pilgrimages!" Since it was my spiritual home, I hadn't really noticed the distance before.

Then, during the summer after my freshman year and the first semester of my sophomore year of college, some huge doors swung wide open. I was called into ministry. I changed schools and majors. I met my wife-to-be in the loan line at the new college. (It was love at first debt.) I received a call to my first pastorate. I was on a new path forward. But I was still a teen and had lots more growing up to do.

What will I do with my life?

Teens wonder about the directions their lives will take and the roads they'll follow to reach their destination. That quest starts early and lasts for a long, long time.

I began to explore the question of "what am I going to be when I grow up" before I became a teen. My second grade year proved pivotal for me under the influence of my teacher, Miss Virginia Lynch. I finally mastered reading and spelling. Then I developed a love for my one-room school's small collection of books on explorers and pioneers. Learning became fun. I looked forward to school and personal exploration.

At the end of that year Miss Lynch announced that she was marrying and moving to another school. My dad, who was president of the school board, and some other community leaders arranged a farewell party for Miss Lynch. During the party's small talk my dad wished Miss Lynch well, and she bragged on me to him. Then she knelt down in front of me so that our faces were on the same plane, and she spoke three or four sentences directly to me. I only remember her empowering final statement: "You can be anything you want to be."

Miss Lynch's blessing and benediction still live in my memory and anchor my soul. That one sentence pointed to doors I didn't know were open. It became an oasis for me.

Remember the affirmation scene from the movie *The Help*, winner of the Best Picture of 2011? With the little girl in her charge sitting in her lap, the nanny quietly says: "You is kind. You is smart. You is important."[5] Then the nanny and little girl smile at each other and repeat that simple message together. The little girl knows that someone believes in her. Isn't it powerful for youngsters to know that an adult values and believes in them?

The "what am I going to be when I grow up" question continues to be a lively issue far beyond our teens and 20s as we explore careers. Although far from finished, these two baseline questions—being and doing—appear in various guises in our teens and 20s. At least, they point us toward "let's try this" tentative responses.

- ☐ Who blessed you?
- ☐ Whom are you blessing?
- ☐ Who is helping you find your niche in the world?

Transitions: Teens to 20s

Leaving our teens creates a life transition. In many cases, stepping into young adulthood is our first major maturity transition. The time has come to find our personal place in the world. We advance on our pathways for faith and maturity. We may still be considered novice adults, but we're on our way.

First, we're leaving our teenaged pre-adult world. College, jobs, the military, and sometimes early marriages separate us from our families of origin. We move out and move on. We build bridges to our adult world.

Second, we enter the adventures of young adulthood. We try on possibilities and make some provisional choices. In our early 20s, life invites us to explore options and turns our young adult years into living experiments. We take on adult responsibilities and search for a comfortable structure for our lives. Our brains mature by our mid-20s and signal it's time to grow up.

Faith has to deepen in order to carry the emerging responsibilities of young adulthood. A teenaged belief system is no longer sturdy enough to support an adult life. Maturity and faith development advance hand-in-hand.

Some teens-to-20s seem to "have it all" early in life; they're what we call "early bloomers." Like gifted athletes and entertainers who peak early, they find success and money quickly and easily. Life is too easy too soon. Early bloomers receive lots of recognition at young ages, and then, when the bloom is gone, they may struggle to find a permanent niche later in life. Though still young in years, those who peak early may soon feel their lives are already behind them. In those cases new goals and purposes, though necessary, become more difficult to find and follow.

All teens-to-20s deal with certain questions related to shaping a "life dream," engaging in a suitable occupation, finding mentors, and establishing lasting relationships.

How can I shape a "life dream"?

Generally a first challenge for 20-somethings is a variation on and an extension of younger hopes raised by our earlier question, "What will I be when I grow up?" In our 20s we begin to shape a life dream that is more defined than a fantasy, more than a "what if" option. On the other hand, at this stage our life dream is less than a carefully thought-out plan. It's a hope, something to try on and test. Our life dream excites us and motivates us to move forward. It's time to explore imagined possibilities.

Dreams call for a new depth of faith. A serious direction in life needs a serious faith anchor to steady it. We may ask ourselves if we really believe. We wonder how to expand our personal faith and values.

My own life dream centers in helping others grow. To prepare for that vocation, I recalled growing crops on the farm and studied psychology and sociology, ethics and theology. I wanted to understand and relate to persons and groups, and I wanted to work with them from a solid moral stance.

As a pastor I realized I had grown into a "people detective" and a practical theologian. As a leadership professor I asked questions of novice ministers to open their imaginations to what they'd need in congregational leadership. One of my students, after he'd served a couple of churches, told me he had learned to learn in my classes. It's a great compliment to know you've helped others become spongy learners in new situations. As director of a leadership center I helped ministers with some leadership experience and a few failures forge new skills and attitudes for their futures.

I've discovered that cultivating plants and working with glass art have helped me see creative progressions and possibilities. Avocations frequently enrich vocations and show connections we would not have eyes to see otherwise.

How can I find an occupation?

In our 20s we face the basic challenge of entering the workplace. We look for work that offers income and, hopefully, meaning. At this life stage we tend to explore careers in an open-ended, trial-and-error fashion. We stay flexible in our workplace explorations and may combine or "hyphenate" occupations. It makes great sense to consider or even to invent blended jobs. After all, we may change careers a half dozen times in our lifetime. So, we look for jobs that morph into other jobs.

Faith explorations undergird occupational searches. Our hunger for meaning pushes us to find the intersections between belief and work. We ask if we can grow from a "God of the gaps" to a "Lord of life" faith.

My early call to ministry was narrowly defined as a result of my past life. I'd only known pastors and missionaries, so I assumed I'd always be one or the other. I began with service in pastoral roles in five very different churches: open country, blue-collar suburban, a new start, white-collar suburban, and a university congregation. Then, my ministry world expanded in unexpected ways when I changed from "retail" to "wholesale" ministry.

I became a pastoral leadership and pastoral care trainer for my national denomination and traveled from coast to coast. I often described that role as a seminary professor without a classroom. Then I actually became a seminary professor, specializing in congregational leadership and building my expertise on the varied types of churches I'd served and seen around our country. Next, I became a denominational executive and directed a leadership center. Now, in retirement, I'm a leadership coach.

Amid all the changes over time, I still see myself as a pastor on loan to the wider church. I'm still discovering ministries for me. In God's hands our callings are always provisional and open-ended.

Who will sponsor me?

As a novice adult we often look for a slightly older guide or encourager—a person with "seniority." These work-related mentors are usually short-term and help us navigate work assignments and on-the-job relationships. Sponsors of both genders support us in our pursuit of our life dream and bolster our confidence.

Faith often involves sponsors too, but a new dimension begins to emerge in our 20s. We wonder if we have a first-hand faith. We ask, "Is my faith my own or Grandma's?"

I've grown because of the support of many sponsors and mentors. I could offer a long list of encouragers in my family and circle of friends. Among the crowd of blessing-givers, I owe more than I can ever repay to people such as Claude McFerron, Ernest Mosley, Randall Lolley, and Reggie McDonough. For instance, Claude "Mac" McFerron was my family's pastor twice during my childhood and teen years. He modeled the Christian life to me, baptized me, and mentored me in my first pastorate. Later he prayed with my mother as she was dying. Mentors such as Mac are priceless.

The best way I can value my mentors' gifts to me is to "pay it forward" by investing in others. You'll see my mentors play starring roles on my life's center stage as my story unfolds in the pages ahead.

Who will love me?

In our 20s we find peers, establish lasting friendships, and cultivate romantic relationships. We may fall in love—repeatedly—until "we get it right." Then we may move ahead to establish marriages and start families.

When we become serious couples or committed mates, we quickly face faith questions:

- ☐ Is my single-person faith mature enough to sustain me as a mate and parent?
- ☐ How can my "me" faith grow into a "we" faith?
- ☐ How can my faith expand to include parenthood?

Our friends, workmates, pastors, spouses, and children love us and make us better. Remember the line from the movie *As Good As It Gets*, "You make me want to be a better man."[6] Love raises our horizons, both freeing and anchoring us.

When Randall Lolley was inaugurated as president of Southeastern Seminary in the 1970s, his father Roscoe was asked to offer the closing prayer. Roscoe, a simple man from southern Alabama, wasn't accustomed to the pomp and ceremony of academic events. Knowing that professors wore robes in formal settings, he asked to wear a suit instead of "a dress." When the ceremony was nearly over and it was his turn to pray, Roscoe, in brief and plain words, simply asked God to give his son "the benefit of the doubt."

That's what loves does. It provides a bit of space for grace, an extra measure of forgiveness, and the benefit of the doubt. Love gives assurances that second chances and new starts will be granted.

Time Out

Near the end of our 20s we generally pause briefly to evaluate how our lives are going. We put everything—our work, relationships, life direction, and faith—on the table for review. It's usually a minor check-up and may not take lots of time, but it allows us to confirm our life course or adjust our headings as needed. Like the flaw in Navajo weavings, it's a time to let the bad out and to invite the good in. It's time to grow up more fully.

A new factor is complicating the typical late-20s time out: student loan debt. For America's college students and graduates, loan debt doubled between 2001 and 2010.[7] By the end of 2009, only mortgages outpaced student debt for American households.

Since the recession of 2007-2008, the student debt load has disrupted the flow of life. The weight of debt has created "late launchers"[8]—young adults who struggle and delay decisions about jobs, marriage, and housing. This emotional and economic burden has made the traditional thresholds of young adulthood more challenging to cross.

The Consultant's Loom

Bob's journey is a beautiful example of how God moves and uses the events of life to accomplish the divine agenda. Every healthy minister I have met shares some similar themes: discovery, imagination, mentors, encouragers, struggle, resilience, and hope.

In my interactions with churches across the country, one specific conversation always emerges. With furrowed brows and a worried tone, they ask: "Where is the next generation of pastoral leadership for churches like ours going to come from?" The concern is based upon a perception that ministry is increasingly seen as a profession that is hard on those who are called to the local church. One resource tells us that 50 percent of ministers leave the ministry within their first five years of service, and that 90 percent of clergy will not make it to retirement from the ministry.[9]

Clearly, anyone entering ministry faces very real and substantial challenges. However, effective and longer tenured clergy have often enjoyed the gifts of a good beginning. Like nearly any profession, early experiences are formative, and strong role models and mentors are invaluable.

For emerging leaders, a strong sense of call, an awareness of core strengths, and an opportunity to explore ministry options in a safe and supportive environment are key ingredients for a meaningful career in ministry. Doing this in the midst of a team of clergy and laity who share common goals and commitments to one another is invaluable.

For me, the privilege of being mentored and guided by men and women across my formative years was a grace-gift that continues to pay dividends in my life, 40 years after sensing the call to ministry. I remain in debt to those who nurtured and affirmed that call in me.

I'm reminded that the great biblical leaders experienced something of the same. Moses received his call on the backside of Midian, but he learned and honed his skills as part of a leadership team with Aaron and others. Saul's dramatic call experience on the road to Damascus led to his being taught and discipled in Saudi Arabia and at the feet of others who saw his potential and worked patiently with him. Jesus clearly saw the value of nurturing new leaders and devoted much of his ministry to getting the disciples and others prepared to carry on when he was no longer physically among them.

Born into a pastor's home, it was natural for me to have ministry as an option for a career. However, I was not initially drawn to ministry and felt led to many other opportunities. Professional baseball was my first choice, but when it became apparent that my skills didn't quite measure up to that calling, I had to reconsider!

It was on a youth mission trip to rural West Virginia that I first took seriously the possibility of a call to ministry. It wasn't my father who voiced that possibility, but our youth minister and my contemporaries who "called me out" and affirmed my potential. That began a multi-year conversation with God and many others as I sought to gain clarity about my calling.

My parents, and especially my father, provided a steady presence across those years of discovery. Dad was a church planter at heart, starting and serving as pastor of just two churches across nearly 40 years of pastoral ministry. Both of those churches started well and remain vibrant and effective today. No one in my life has ever modeled what it means to be a healthy minister like my father. I just assumed all ministers were the kind of man my father was: putting family first, humble, full of integrity, honest, loyal, positive, devoted to Christ, in love with the church, believing the best about people. Only later did I discover what an exception he was. He and my mother were in love with one another and showed my sisters and me what it meant to be a healthy family. Thankfully, I started with a positive role model and inspiration that continue to drive me today as I work to help congregations and clergy become what God intends them to be.

With that positive experience as a background orientation, I began to think deeply about giving my life to this vocation called ministry. If that was what a minister looked like, I could only hope to emulate something of that in my life.

People such as Frank Hart Smith, Jim Poole, Dewey Jones, Lloyd and Masako Cornell, Ira Peak, Ruby Treadway, Bill and Rebecca Whittaker, Tom and Rita Moody, Robert and Jean Wooddy, Randy and Betty Smith, Ray

Conner, and Don and Kathy Mattingly all spoke into my life and took an interest in me. Gradually I found myself given opportunities and appropriate coaching as I found my voice and discovered my gifts.

Upon graduation from seminary I was invited to join the ministerial team at a large church and continue my transition into the emerging leader phase of my ministry. There I found mentors and friends, both laity and clergy, who nurtured me and provided opportunities to grow and to learn what it meant to be an effective minister. Some of those lessons were exhilarating, and some were excruciating. All were valuable.

Healthy churches and clergy are concerned about creating a congregational culture that encourages call and supports and nurtures those who view their vocation as a mission and not simply as a means to an income. I am so encouraged by the movement in many churches to invite members to consider more deeply than ever before the implications of a healthy "theology of call" upon their educational and vocational choices.

The Pathways to Ministry residency program at Wilshire Baptist Church in Dallas, funded by a Lilly grant, is probably the finest example of a church taking seriously its role in maturing our emerging generation of leaders.[10] Many of their insights can be found in a superb book written by Wilshire's pastor, George Mason.[11] This residency program illustrates well the profound impact of voices of thoughtful encouragement (think Barnabas!) in the call process.

I grew up hearing a weekly invitation issued at the close of worship that consisted of four components:

1. Respond to the call to become a Christian.
2. Join our church.
3. Rededicate your life to Christ.
4. Consider giving yourself to "full-time Christian service."

As a pastor and coach to clergy and churches, I have found few congregations overtly calling their constituents to consider decisions regarding renewal of faith and/or vocation. What if those two are fused together and comprise one of the richest opportunities for 21st century churches to impact their community for the good of the Kingdom?

One congregation I served took the Hannah / Eli / Samuel narrative and turned it into a structured process of inviting young people to explore making their educational and vocational choices through the lens of "calling." The result was profound. Nearly every participant reported that having conversations about college and vocational decisions led them to make different and/or more satisfying choices. Several chose to pursue ministry, but all reported a deeper understanding of how God could use them and their vocations for the good of the Kingdom.

Integrating faith into the educational and vocational life of young adults is at the heart of a church that is relevant and vital in the 21st century. Many books and organizations are emerging to help us create a more coherent and relevant way of thinking about God's dream and our vocational dream. Weaving those strands together will help us avoid the all-too-frequent malady of a life built in silos, missing that key connecting theme of providential grace and vision.

Our Try-and-Fly Decades

Since crafting leaders of faith is a learn-by-doing art, young leaders in churches and religious organizations need a rich array of life laboratories. Religious arenas for leaders in the try-and-fly decades include a number of options, such as the following:

- internships
- residencies
- apprenticeships
- mentorships
- cross-cultural and language immersions
- faith formation retreats
- tours of working ministries
- traveling seminars
- participation in cohort groups

Young leaders bloom in on-the-job training as they try on life and mature in their faith.

Our teens and 20s afford almost two decades of discovery. Hopefully in these decades we find our niches for life's contribution over time, take part in communities of faith discovery and leader practice, find ways to transform ourselves and others, and learn to live bigger, more redemptive stories. Rather than simply making a living, we search for ways to make and remake lives for ourselves and for others. We want to leave our fingerprints on God's work in the world.

We need to ask ourselves what we have mastered and what we have missed. When basic issues for this life stage aren't clarified and an adult level of maturity attained, some catch-up work is necessary. The good news is that there's time to lay foundations for ourselves and move forward.

In our teens and 20s we can find ourselves and launch our lives. We've experimented with and tested an array of options. We are now moving beyond our try-and-fly decades. It's time to transition into our 30s and to weave some additional foundation threads into the fabric of our lives and faith.

Leaders Moving Forward

Younger leaders in their teens and 20s bring lots of energy and a spirit of exploration into workplaces and faith communities. Now, at the end of our 20s, we're active in the leadership arena and gaining experience for larger service. As people of faith we're updating our beliefs and behaviors for the demands of adult responsibilities.

We're weaving our lives, faiths, and futures. What's still ahead?

Notes

[1] Tania Lombrozo, "3 Things Everyone Should Know Before Growing Up," National Public Radio, 30 June 2014.

[2] Robert D. Dale, *Memories of the Future: A Memoir of Virginia Baptists' Young Leaders' Program* (Richmond, VA: Center for Baptist Heritage and Studies, 2009).

[3] The life cycle and its challenges have been described by psychologists in various constructs. Readers of this book will recognize the formative ideas of Erik H. Erikson, et. al. *Psychological Issues*, vol. 1 (International Universities Press, 1959); Frederic M. Hudson, *The Adult Years: Mastering the Art of Self-Renewal* (San Francisco: Jossey-Bass Publishers, 1991); Daniel J. Levinson, et. al., *The Seasons of a Man's Life* (New York: Alfred A. Knopf, 1978); Daniel J. and Judy D. Levinson, *The Seasons of a Woman's Life* (New York: Random House, 1997); Dan P. McAdams, *Stories We Live By: Personal Myths and the Making of the Self* (New York: William Morrow and Co., 1993).

[4] My family espoused the "frontier thesis," the idea that expanding and settling the western frontier molded American character profoundly. Historian Frederick Jackson Turner's 1891 essay, "The Significance of the Frontier in American History," established the frontier thesis and made Turner the leading historian of the frontier, brought young historians under his influence, and created a long-term conversation about the frontier among historians.

[5] From Tate Taylor's film adaptation, *The Help*, 2011.

[6] *As Good As It Gets* (TriStar Pictures, 1997) received Academy Awards for Best Actor, Jack Nicholson, and Best Actress, Helen Hunt.

[7] Richard Fry, "Young Adults, Student Debt, and Economic Well-Being," Pew Research on Social and Demographic Trends, http://www.pewsocialtrends.org/2014/05/14/young-adults-student-debt-and-economic-well-being.

[8] Steve Rosen, "Young Adults Are Feeling Strain of Student Loan Debt," Richmond (VA) *Times-Dispatch*, 18 July 2014, D4.

[9] http://www.expastors.com/why-do-so-many-pastors-leave-the-ministry-the-facts-will-shock-you/; http://www.pastorburnout.com/pastor-burnout-statistics.html; https://docs.google.com/viewer?url=http%3A%2F%2Fwww.oak.edu%2F~oakedu%2Fassets%2Fck%2Ffiles%2FStewart%2B(SU%2B09).pdf.

[10] http://www.wilshirebc.org/learn/pathways-to-ministry/.

[11] George A. Mason, *Preparing the Pastors We Need: Reclaiming the Congregation's Role in Training Clergy* (Lanham, MD: Rowman and Littlefield, 2002). http://www.amazon.com/gp/product/1566994276?keywords=george%20mason%20alban%20press&qid=1450880172&ref_=sr_1_fkmr0_1&s=books&sr=1-1-fkmr0.

"Hustle" Threads
Leader Maturity for 30s and 40s

Our 30s and 40s usher us into full adulthood. We're no longer novice adults who automatically are given some slack just because we're young. Now we're wearing our "big boy" or "big girl" pants. We're in the mainstream decades finally. We're expected to hustle and contribute.

Leaders at Full Gallop

The Bible often shows life lived "at full gallop." Remember how frazzled Moses became as the Hebrews' leader in the wilderness (Exodus 18)? His father-in-law, Jethro, brought Moses' family back to him—a painful reminder of Moses' personal overload. During the visit Jethro learned about God's work and watched Moses referee disputes during a long and wearing day. Out of concern for Moses' health, Jethro counseled Moses to share the burdens of judging disagreements. Moses saw the wisdom of Jethro's suggestions and adopted his plan. Delegating responsibilities, Moses only served as the appeals judge for the most difficult cases—easing some of the "hustle."

Doctor Phil on television often asks a direct question: "How's that working for you?" It's a timely inquiry for us to ask ourselves as we approach age 30. It's a good time to assess our life direction and spiritual progress.

Our transition into our 30s begins with a pause to assess how our lives are going. We're beginning to see that life oscillates back and forth between seasons of stability and seasons of change.[1] We need to be clear about what's working for us and what isn't.

With better answers from our 20s and a bit more perspective on life and faith, we can take stock and make decisions.

☐ If we're moving in the right direction, we can continue to move ahead smoothly and speedily.

☐ If we're slightly off-track, we can slow down, fine-tune our direction, and then proceed forward.

☐ If we're going the wrong way, we can stop, turn around, and reset our compasses for more productive headings.

In any case, we know that real adults are expected to "get it right." In our 30s it's our time to stand at center stage of life and faith.

Settling In

Modern culture views 30-somethings as full-fledged adults rather than junior adults. The demands of adulthood now rest squarely on our shoulders. Whether the transition to our 30s was easy and smooth or stressful and crisis-filled, the time has come to move on and settle in.

We're finding our niche and progressing on our timetable. More is expected of us at this life stage, and we're positioning ourselves to deliver. Still, we have more questions to face, more cultivating of self and soul to do. We seek stability for our lives, career advancement, balance between life and work, and a voice that is our own.

How can I stabilize and root my life?

Our 30s continue some of the rapid start-and-stop cadence of our 20s. We move fast at work, at home, at church—all at the same time. We complicate our lives by acquiring lots of things in our 30s—marriages, children, homes, friends, more debts, investments, and leisure "toys." In the whirlwind we depend on our faith, family, friends, and support networks to stabilize and keep us upright—much like the central taproot of a tree.

After a season of rapid change and transition, we lean on life structure to anchor us. We're developing an "internal gyroscope,"[2] a personal calling and maturing faith, to orient and guide us. This inner gyroscope makes the world seem a bit safer to us, a bit less unmoored. We become a bit more trusting of our own judgment and instincts and a bit less panicky when we stumble. We've learned enough from our transitions and changes to move us into stable seasons with more confidence.

Frankly, I was tired of the sprint of being 20-something. In my 20s I'd finished college, gotten married, served three churches, and had completed two seminary degrees. I was eager to settle into permanent adulthood, if that's what my 30s would bring. I was ready to put down roots and be a full contributor to God's kingdom.

I hadn't discovered yet that life's chapters keep turning their pages quickly. I had no clue that my life and work would take off and fly high during the first half of my 30s and then crash and burn in my late 30s.

How well am I progressing in my career?

The life dream that began to emerge in our earlier years takes fuller, crisper definition in our 30s. After all, we're climbing the ladder. For many of us, work dominates this decade. The structures in our lives fit better and feel more comfortable. Our life dream energizes us, and we move to make it unfold smoothly. There's a niche for us and a sequence that makes sense to us. Life seems lined up now.

When I was 30 years old my ministry career moved in a new direction and took on a new stability. I had experience in four diverse churches already, had finished my doctorate, and had become hungry for continuity in my life, family, and work. That summer I became pastor of the First Southern Baptist Church in Lawrence, Kansas.

Still a young congregation, the church was located directly across the street from the University of Kansas, with dorms and married student housing in view of our site. We were just down the street from Allen Field-house, the famed sports and event arena where the inventor of basketball, James Naismith, had once coached. This unique church was a rare blend of congregational types, both an "Old First" and a university church. It was also a balanced town-gown congregation, with roughly half of the members from the city and half from the university community.

For the first time in my ministry I was in a church where I could see myself staying for the rest of my life. Although I didn't stay in Lawrence forever, the feeling that I had found a ministry home was new, assuring, and stabilizing. My emotional and spiritual root system was maturing and growing downward.

As I settled into a pastoral routine I found ways to grow personally and professionally. I took classes at the university and in the school of religion, joined a professional support group, got involved in an ecumenical consulting network, wrote a regular column for the Baptist newspaper, created a marriage enrichment ministry, found new ways to balance my sermon themes, and became a father. My life and career were growing upward. I had found my place. I was running a hundred miles an hour, stretched to the limit but loving it all.

How am I dealing with life-work balance?

In our 30s work-life balance also becomes tougher. Marriages, families, jobs, health, and faith get stretched. To up the ante, our 30s are often our busiest and most exhausting life decade. When we become over-pressured, personal and professional development often take a back seat to the chaos of daily living.

In our late 30s we may wonder if younger competitors are gaining on us. Time and age become factors for us in a new way. We don't want to be passed up in the race when midlife is looming up on the horizon.

At age 33 after three years in the Lawrence pastorate, my career took a surprising turn. I had attended a large gathering of university students in Norman, Oklahoma, and sat in on a training session taught by Ernest Mosley, leader of the new pastoral ministry work for Southern Baptists. After the session Ernest and I introduced ourselves, chatted a bit, had dinner together, and got better acquainted. He surprised me at the end of the meal by offering me a nation-wide training job in pastoral leadership and pastoral care. I was stunned by two issues: We'd only just met, and, typical of young adults of the 1960s and 1970s, I'd complained a lot about national denominational trends. Of course, I didn't really know "them," but I wasn't sure I wanted to become a turncoat and work with and for "them."

But the deeper issue for me was a matter of scale and focus. I'd always seen myself only as a local church pastor, probably as a country preacher. Now, Ernest was asking me to move from "retail" to "wholesale." I couldn't see a future for me in Nashville.

I called home and laughingly told my wife about Ernest's offer. I fully expected her to make light of the national ministry possibility. Instead, she listened carefully as I described the new job. Then, while I was still chuckling, she said, "This is what you've been getting ready to do all your life. You just didn't know where to look for the opportunity." I was stopped in my tracks. Suddenly I knew she was right. I'd already served five very different churches in four states.[3] Without having the gumption to see it, God was preparing me to work with ministers who served all types of churches in a variety of settings. Although still young, I'd already "been there and done that."

So, I became a pastor on loan to my denomination. I moved from a busy pastorate to a teaching ministry in a different place every week. The job was like being a professor with a mobile classroom. I focused on pastoral leadership, then an emerging discipline, and pastoral care, generally a strong point in the Baptist tradition. It was exciting and enjoyable work. Barnstorming in the old open-cockpit biplanes: that's the way I described my innovative work role. Our pastoral ministries team's new work allowed me to specialize, a rare luxury in ministry. I savored the gift. This role stretched me toward a new flexibility and a new type of faith for specialization.

But my life soon got out of balance. I had two young children, my wife was overloaded, and I was living in airplanes. After I'd spent four years on the road my preschool son pointed to the airport's flight line one morning and innocently asked me "which plane I owned." As my young family waited for me to exit Nashville's air terminal after another trip, my son asked his mother "Is that Daddy?" several times as other male travelers approached along the sidewalk. From the mouth of a babe, those words signaled to me that I wasn't present enough to be a good dad and husband. Maybe as a result of living as a frequent flyer, I detest airline travel to this day.

Not only was I absent from home too much, but I was also overly stressed, a trigger for the development of some health issues. I began having trouble maintaining a consistent energy level. I was exhausting my adrenal glands and sliding into Type 2 diabetes. It was time to find a ministry that was more humane for my family and my body. I wasn't being a good family leader, and I wasn't taking care of my health. My life and spirit had grown lopsided and out of balance. I was forced to develop a faith that slowed the blur of life. I needed both anchors and elasticity.

How am I finding my voice?

When we find our own voice, we feel more at home in our own skins, more independent. We trust our expertise more. We take fuller possession of our personalities and strengths. For the first time we recognize and appreciate the authority of our own voice. When we find our voice and gain perspective, our humor tends to become more philosophical and self-deprecating. Additionally, we often jettison our mentors—a key sign that we're confident of and comfortable in our life position. Although this parting is frequently painful, it's a natural process. Until about age 40 we need mentors to amplify our voices. After 40 we become mentors to others.

I found my public voice in the pulpit during my early 30s. Humor was my clue that I had my own voice. I'd grown up in a mountain story-telling culture in which preachers stood up, read their texts, prayed, told a joke, and then preached. It always seemed odd and artificial to me that they inserted a random joke between the biblical text and the sermon on that text. Telling jokes in the pulpit wasn't my style.

But I knew I'd found my voice when I could be naturally funny in the pulpit without manufacturing a joke. I'd always known that I "think funny" and that I was often smiling internally. Then I saw that humor is God's way of giving us perspective about life. From that point forward, humor flowed easily into my observations on life and theology. I preached a sermon series on Jesus' emotions, including laughter. In the sermon I used the story Jesus told the Pharisees about swallowing camels (Matt. 23:24). I described the process of swallowing a hoof, hairy shin, and calloused knee. I'm sure Jesus intended to bring a smile to the Pharisees' faces and to widen their humorless perspective, but it didn't. And 20 centuries later, some members of my congregation weren't sure Jesus was funny either. Still, I saw and continue to see humor as a sign of emotional and spiritual health. In any event, humor showed me that I'd become comfortable in my own skin, could demonstrate that comfort in church, and had a voice to use.

At age 37 I became professor of pastoral leadership, the first in my denomination, at Southeastern Baptist Theological Seminary in Wake Forest, North Carolina. At my age and stage, Randall Lolley, the seminary president, put lots of faith in me. I taught young ministers to practice different leadership styles, to diagnose the health of congregations, to deal creatively with conflict and change, and to assess their callings and career directions. My most popular course was "Survival Skills for Ministers." I also directed the doctoral program. Teaching leadership and leading an academic program were perfect fits for me. I had found my place and my voice in the classroom.

A seminary faculty is a unique collection of specialists, a diverse group of experts who just happen to have offices in the same building. Everyone is a leader in his or her own niche. I once described faculty meetings in pastoral terms: like a deacon's meeting where everyone's the chairperson. As both a teacher and an administrator, I sometimes felt I was caught in no-man's land between individual authorities and different interests.

Sadly, in my second semester at seminary, my health worsened. My body was sabotaging me. I couldn't count on steady energy levels. I lost an entire summer from memory. Travel and freelance preaching became nearly impossible. I was scared. Ironically, I was finally in a professional post that fit me like a glove, and I was about to lose my ministry opportunity.

Then, an old habit served my teaching ministry in new ways. As a pastor I'd developed the practice of using my preaching preparations in at least two ways. It was stewardship of the hard work of sermon preparation. Now I began to use my teaching preparation for writing purposes. Maybe I couldn't roam and preach, but with discipline I could write at least a publishable page each day. That habit produced a book and a half, along with numerous journal articles and magazine columns, each year for a dozen years. The folks at Broadman Press described my *To Dream Again* as the most important book they published in the 1980s.[4] I had a voice on paper. Even better, writing became a portable ministry resource that traveled to places I couldn't go.

Carpe Diem: Late Peakers and Midlifers

In the second half of our 30s some of us who have struggled and lagged behind in early adulthood get momentum. These "late peakers," the opposite of those who peak early, now make up for lost time. Some have taken time off and now re-engage. Some have simply awakened to opportunity. Women, if they have delayed their careers for family responsibilities, may now rise to the top quickly. Entrepreneurs who have waited and timed their markets well may finally have their moment in the sun.

Midlife happens to all of us. Somewhere in our late 30s or around age 40 life turns a corner. Our midlife transition can be a major time-out for us. Along with this major evaluation there's an ominous sense of mortality. We wonder if the "bloom is off the rose" and question our youth.

Like many of life's transitions, midlife can be either a loss or an opportunity.

If we define midlife as *loss*—the less likely option—we may experience a "midlife crisis." We may feel a general unrest, and fear a "crash and burn" event is upon us. Negatively, we're forced to discover who we are and to put our lives back together. We may reconcile "young" versus "old," energy versus experience. Positively, we try to bring better balance to our lives. We may evaluate our relationships, faith, and careers—and then renew or exit. We search inwardly to live outwardly.

On the other hand, if we view midlife as *opportunity*—the more likely option—we may use our introspection to become more self-aware and to grow quickly. We may gain balance in our personality and moderate the extremes inside us. We may put creativity in the spotlight. We may expand the reach of our generosity. Our relationships may deepen. We may become stronger nurturers of our children as well as better stewards of our service opportunities and our mentoring relationships. We may contribute more at home and work. Maybe the old saying has some truth and life does begin at 40.

Hurdles for 40-Somethings

In broad strokes, midlife sends genders in distinctive directions. Women are seen as connected and interdependent. Men are seen as separate and independent.[5] Past midlife, both genders are now "in charge." We have more experience than those who are younger and more energy than those who are older, which is a resilient combination. But questions still abound about our personal and professional growth and about our relationships with different family members.

How am I growing now?

Our 40s give us a chance to continue to grow. In our 20s we are generalists, exploring a world of options. In our 30s we specialize in perfecting personal and professional roles. Then, in our 40s we become generalists in ourselves. We become more reflective. We sort, simplify, prune, and make choices. We draw or redraw our boundaries. We have a chance to take possession of our best selves.

Frederic Hudson offers a wise word of warning: "Repossessing your soul without wrecking your life is not always easy."[6] Repossessing our souls raises some tough questions:

- ☐   Is my faith deepening and expanding?
- ☐   Are my relationships being enriched?
- ☐   Am I cultivating personal skills for new challenges?
- ☐   Am I investing more time and energy in leisure and non-work activities?

I was granted a study leave from the seminary when I was 43. That year I served on the staff of the Center for Creative Leadership in Greensboro, North Carolina, the world's top-ranked leadership resource. I needed the center's extensive and specialized library holdings to write a book on leader styles.[7] Staff there asked me to help global leaders deal with family pressures and to cope with bribery attempts. It was a productive and interesting year. It was prime time to reflect, stretch, and grow.

This study leave was a timely change of pace for me both personally and professionally. Personally, it was a time to make progress in regaining my health. I was able to create my own schedule, pace myself, and exercise more. I took charge of recovering my energy and strength. Professionally, I saw the inside of leadership testing and training processes for business, military, and not-for-profit leaders. That perspective broadened and enriched my horizons. I grew in new directions.

Where is my career taking me?

As we rise through the work ranks in our 40s we may move into more important leadership roles. We focus more on quality than quantity. We discover that some of our professional skills and training need updating. We wonder if we can work another 20 to 30 years—or if we want to. We begin to consider "encore or bridge careers," less stressful jobs that we do mostly for satisfaction and contribution. Or, to respond to Bob Buford's insight, we question if we have pursued success long enough and are now ready to look for significance.[8] Around "halftime," our focus turns from perpetual motion to personal meaning.

In my 40s I was certainly looking for meaning and significance in my calling. But within a couple of years of settling into the seminary's routines, my denomination became deeply divided by political and theological strife. A takeover at the top of the denomination was underway. The seminaries were major targets for the reformers. New trustees for the seminaries were chosen for their political views. One new trustee at Southeastern thought seminaries taught Old Testament, New Testament, and nothing else. When I gave him one of my books on leadership he was completely flummoxed. Apparently, teaching leadership didn't fit his idea of ministerial training.

The mood on campus turned hostile. Faculty and trustees had traditionally worked closely as partners in theological education. Now the trustees stopped speaking to faculty members and treated us like enemies of the faith. Students were enlisted to spy in the classrooms. Trustees investigated several of my teaching colleagues to see if they were orthodox. Our entire executive team resigned in protest of the attacks. In that tense atmosphere I had a much better sense of what the Old Testament exile must have felt like to the Hebrews.

In the midst of the painful turmoil I was largely spared from direct attack. Because I was a "practical" theologian who was known for my books and conference work, no one was trying to fire me. I was considered "safe." In fact, some of the attackers made it a point to assure me that I was a productive and protected teacher. But I quickly knew I didn't want to work in the hostile or unappreciative setting that was evolving at Southeastern. At age 47 I took a half sabbatical and enrolled in a local clinical psychology degree program. I wanted to be sure I could continue to invest my gifts and experiences in others. I wanted to be sure I could feed and shelter my family. I began to consider my next steps.

How am I relating to different generations?

In our 40s it's natural to see that our children and our parents are both facing life transitions. We have to expand our parenting skills to relate well to teen and young adult children. Our parents are coping with life and aging challenges and may be looking to us for assistance. Professionally, we may find ourselves working with or supervising employees with generational differences that we don't fully understand.

Generational dynamics remain lively throughout life. When at age 49 I left a tenured professorship at the invitation of Reggie McDonough for a ministry with the Virginia Mission Board in Richmond, we kept our two children's transitions on the front edge of our planning.

My wife and I fretted that the negative atmosphere created by the seminary's trustees would scar our son and daughter's feelings about and connections to churches. Our son was moving into college, a natural transition in itself. But between her sophomore and junior years in high school, our daughter was being moved away from lifelong friends and the only schools she'd known. We decided to do something we hadn't considered before. We let our daughter choose our church in Richmond. She selected well and had many of the same friends at school and at church. To this day she's a key leader in her own church. Thank goodness, the seminary experience didn't deter our children from faith.

The Consultant's Loom

I suspect that the largest percentage of clergy our Center for Healthy Churches works with fall into the "Hustle" category. Mid-career ministers are at a unique, multifaceted, and highly demanding moment in their careers. It is a time to maximize their skills and lean into their strengths, and profound self-discovery can occur in this season of ministry.

Like Bob, I found myself in a constant state of self-discovery during this portion of ministry. It seemed that every week I read a book, attended a conference, or watched a video that both challenged me and forced me to realize how much I didn't know about what I was trying to do and be.

After my own chaotic sprint through my 20s and into my early 30s, the single most helpful thing I did was to begin a journey inward that sought to balance what I knew about myself with what I knew about ministry. I could talk at length about how to do ministry, but I mostly needed help with how to be me. So began a time of exploring my family of origin and my role in it, examining my deepest motivations, and ruthlessly assessing my failures and successes. It all blended together to create a season of rich discernment and insight. I found help from fellow clergy, counselors, coaches, and family members. I rediscovered God's call upon my life and found myself more engaged in my life as a husband, father, and minister in a much healthier fashion.

This hard work of self-reflection and discernment is nearly impossible to do alone. When you invite others into the conversation, new dimensions of insight are possible that were previously hidden from you. Healthy clergy discover the power of mentors, spiritual directors, coaches, and therapists as sources of light into the dark corners of their soul.

While this season of ministry presents challenges to clergy, our 30s and 40s also give us numerous growth opportunities. Consider the following:

☐ Explore your family of origin, and the inevitable anxiety you carry.

☐ Begin to appreciate the power of authentic humility.

☐ Cultivate the ability to manage polarities.

☐ Learn adaptive leadership methods and how to climb your own leadership tower.

☐ Become a builder of trust in the leadership culture.

☐ Take seriously your role as a "trust accelerator."

☐ Provide inspiration and motivation to colleagues and parishioners.

☐ Enhance your ability to self-reflect, seek out a "Nathan," and build your own emotional intelligence.

☐ Exercise biblical stewardship principles with regard to your time, talents, attention, and energy.

☐ Target areas for deliberate and intentional growth.

☐ Cultivate the capacity to disagree agreeably and to lean into conflict.

☐ Bring vision clarity and become a "chief articulator of the vision."

☐ Relentlessly align your life and that of your congregation with your stated personal mission.

☐ Serve as chief talent scout, and think extensively about replicating leaders.

☐ Live out of an abundance mentality.

☐ Pay attention to the invisible people, events, emotions, motives, and desires around you.

☐ Be disciplined about self-care and your devotional core.

Finding ourselves and creating a clearer focus around God's specific call and talent set in our life is a critical task for the "Hustle" pastor. Being all things to all people not only doesn't ever happen, but it also feeds into exhaustion and burnout. Being able to winnow out our deepest passions and calling is a powerful experience for this season of ministry. I hope you find your way toward that unique insight.

Finishing Our Burning-and-Turning Decades

Our 30s and 40s are our burning-and-turning decades. Amid our busy-ness, we've checked our progress in life and made course corrections. We may have reinvented ourselves in some ways. We've searched for new relational styles with spouses, children, and parents. We've tried to rebalance our personal and work lives.

We've grown up and matured, whether we're working or relaxing. As Peter Drucker discovered, we may have found some growth and future career possibilities in our hobby or leisure interests. Drucker believed that a leader's best contribution is that of a "mature person—and you cannot have maturity if you have no life or interest outside the job."[9]

We've hustled, burned candles at both ends, and turned corners at midlife. We're now established leaders.

We've entered "Life II"[10] by our mid-40s. We've begun a different, a second, life season of adulthood. Now we have to manage the sweat equity in our lives in new ways for the future as we transition to bigger challenges.

With four decades of life and experience under our belts, we can now harness our energy and experience into a specific calling. We're beginning to think, believe, and lead more strategically. We're poised for life's larger arenas. Our faith has become more reflective and grounded. We've woven the lessons of four decades together.

At this stage we've mastered many of life's developmental demands. We may still need to complete some of the hurdles we haven't cleared. We likely need to update our faith pilgrimage for new challenges.

There's more to come. As we approach 50, what's ahead for us?

Notes

[1] Frederic M. Hudson, *The Adult Years: Mastering the Art of Self-Renewal* (San Francisco: Jossey-Bass, 1991), 66-70.

[2] Ibid., 184-185.

[3] I had served as pastor of Clear Creek Baptist Church, Pierce City, Missouri (a family chapel congregation in the open countryside); youth minister at Birchman Avenue Baptist Church, Fort Worth, Texas (a traditional blue-collar suburban church); pastor of Joy Chapel, Wynnewood, Oklahoma (a new mission start-up); associate pastor at Royal Lane Baptist Church, Dallas, Texas (an upscale white-collar suburban church); and pastor of First Southern Baptist Church, Lawrence, Kansas (a combination Old First / university congregation). Later I served as interim pastor at Rowan Baptist Church, Clinton, North Carolina (a community church on the outskirts of a small town).

[4] Robert D. Dale, *To Dream Again: How to Help Your Church Come Alive* (Nashville: Broadman Press, 1981).

[5] Hudson, *The Adult Years*, 155.

[6] Ibid., 162.

[7] Robert D. Dale, *Ministers as Leaders* (Nashville: Broadman Press, 1984).

[8] Bob Buford, *Half Time: Changing Your Game Plan from Success to Significance* (Grand Rapids: Zondervan, 1994).

[9] Bruce Rosenstein, *Living in More Than One World: How Peter Drucker's Wisdom Can Inspire and Transform Your Life* (San Francisco: Berrett-Koehler Publishers, 2009), 15-21.

[10] Bob Buford, *Finishing Well: What People Who REALLY Live Do Differently!* (Nashville: Integrity Publishers, 2004), xiii.

"Legacy" Threads
Leader Maturity for 50s and 60s

Our 50s and 60s are our legacy decades. We wonder what we'll leave behind for younger generations to build on. It's that pesky old question, "What do I want on my gravestone?" To create a permanent stewardship is a sobering thought.

Legacy becomes a practical test of our integrity. We search for our deepest and most authentic contribution, without dilution or detours. If some of our dreams remain untried, now is the time to relax the reins and let that pony run.

What will we invest in for the long haul? To add to the pressure, time is now of the essence. It's our last chance to make a mark and to pass it along to future generations. It's our best chance to bequeath a "symbolic immortality"[1] to later leaders.

At this life stage we're grown up enough to live and give generously. We can model the way forward for others, and we can mentor them. We can extend blessings to others. We can "reimagine our lives."[2] We can look for ways to invest in the future through at least four channels:

- [ ] Family—How are my children doing in life?
- [ ] Work—How am I growing enough to make an impact on my 9-5 workplace?
- [ ] Service—How will my faith-filled concerns for others define me?
- [ ] Time—How many years do I have to make a difference?

Framing Our 50s

Our fifth decade on earth raises even more serious growth challenges than the earlier ones. We feel the hourglass beginning to empty and realize we have to make good use of whatever time we have left. It's high time to begin living and giving—and to ask some hard questions about our legacy in the present and future and of how we relate to and care for others.

What kind of legacy will I leave?

We could ask ourselves a variety of questions regarding the issue of legacy, for example:

☐   What have I done with my life?

☐   What will I leave behind when I'm gone?

☐   When stories are told about me, what will be said?

☐   Which churches and volunteer organizations will remember me?

☐   Which of my ideas will live on?

The answers to these inquiries tend to cluster around three themes:

1. **Legacy is invested in our children and the people we've mentored.** The people we have shaped deeply are likely to carry our values forward. We see our life principles and the impact of our mentoring in them, and we take pride in their accomplishments. We celebrate their victories and take satisfaction in their milestones. We take joy in watching them pay it forward.

2. **Legacy is reflected in the direct influences we've had on others.** The ways we've served in our various environments—at home, at work, in our communities of faith and residency, and for different causes—are mirrored by this special network. Upon retirement my wife and I evaluated our gifts of money beyond our church tithe. We discovered that our hearts were stirred by others' needs in four arenas: hunger, housing, health, and hopes for futures. We began systematically to give to local organizations such as the Ronald McDonald House and key medical research groups. I also volunteered for several clinical studies designed to test and develop medical drugs.

3. **Legacy is shown by our gifts to people and needs.** When I retired I gave away 90 percent of my professional library. I gave my children first choice. Then I identified five persons with unusual potential. I believed in them and their ministries. One after the other, they came to my office and selected books that appealed to them. Although these books were professional treasures and "virtual friends," I felt no sense of loss. Rather, the books were personal gifts and continued investments in my key ministry partners. I didn't tell my book selectors the larger story, but I'd experienced this kind of generosity myself as a young minister. R. A. Hutson, an interim pastor in my parents' church in Missouri, invited me to his home office and gave me a dozen or so books. As he handed each one to me, he

made a formal introduction about the book and talked about what it had taught him and how the author had enriched his ministry. It was a holy moment. I felt Elijah's mantle had been draped over my shoulders for the journey ahead.

At age 50 I saw an old pattern in a new way. My last three ministry roles—in Nashville, at Wake Forest, and in Richmond—were all brand new niches. No one had done these jobs before me. As a result I discovered what a unique opportunity it is to be the "first," the "founder," and the creator of molds for others. Like my Grandpa Kingry before me, I was a homesteader who took risks and opened new frontiers. It's a holy moment when you can open new doors for other leaders.

In Richmond I took a new role with the Virginia Baptist Mission Board supervising a team of gifted leaders who worked with Baptist ministers across the Commonwealth. We were leaders for leaders, pastors of pastors. One aspect of this new job was to develop a leadership center, an extension of the work I'd done in Nashville and at Wake Forest. It was an enjoyable opportunity to expand opportunities for other leaders in the Virginia Baptist family.

How can I transition from a "me life" to a "we life"?

During the first half of our lives we concentrate on ourselves and our smaller worlds of family and work. In the second half of life we begin to experience interdependence and discover how we can impact the larger world and how it shapes us. We move from "me" to "we."[3]

I'd been focused on my own health for 15 years when my next-younger brother Jim got sick. My "me" world was about to expand to "we" in short order. During the spring of 1992 Jim couldn't shake off an infection. After several weeks of medical tests, local doctors in southwestern Colorado still couldn't figure out what was happening to him. They sent him to a medical center in Denver for a more extensive battery of tests.

My own family was in Missouri in June to celebrate my grandmother's 100th birthday with the extended Dale clan. I called Jim to check on him since he couldn't join us for the party. I heard something in his voice that concerned me. When I asked what I was sensing he admitted, "I'm giving up." I told him to hang on a bit longer. Reinforcements were on the way.

That conversation was the beginning of the most significant gift I've given to anyone so far. The next day I went to Denver with my wife and children. Soon we learned that Jim had leukemia and needed a bone marrow transplant. Tests showed that he and I were almost twins genetically. I was his best donor.

During the fall of 1992 I spent eight weeks with Jim at Seattle's cluster of hospitals on "Pill Hill," preparing for the transplant that was then an experimental procedure. Jim and I had been together only occasionally and briefly at family gatherings over more than 20 years. When we left home he had moved west, I'd migrated east, and we'd mostly lost touch. But we had unhurried heart-to-heart conversations in the hospital and quickly found we were alike in many more ways than just genetics. It was good to get a brother back. It was even better to offer a life-saving gift.

Jim's transplant happened successfully in November. The cancer was finally gone. Jim returned home to Colorado later in the spring and by summer was getting ready to go back to his job with the school district. One morning in mid-August he had a toothache from an infected tooth. With a still-weakened immune system, the abscess spread to his brain and killed him within a week.

I had found a brother and then lost him. In the process I learned a lesson common to those of us in our fifth decade: It's a "we" world, and that discovery calls for generosity. At this life stage we begin to pay it forward freely and deliberately.

How am I dealing with being the "sandwich generation"?

When we become involved in the care of our children and our parents we're in a generational sandwich. Whether our children are at home, in school, or away for a job or military service, they're still a part of our family circle. Different parenting skills have to be developed and matched to new parenting demands. We begin to learn how to let go, how to launch them well. At the same time our elders are aging and may need some extra care. It's difficult to look back, look ahead, and pay much attention to our own challenges—all simultaneously.

A call from my dad when I was in my early 50s changed our relationship. Dad had always been a strict taskmaster. I had once gotten an "A-" on an otherwise "straight-A" report card, and Dad insisted that I do better right now! He was one of those "as long as you put your feet under my dining table, you live by my rules" guys. Even when he was proud of me, he couldn't find ways to say so. Dad was always the parent, and I was always the little kid in his eyes.

Then, Dad called one night to tell me he'd been diagnosed with diabetes. Since I'd been a diabetic for nearly 20 years by then, he asked my advice. He wanted to understand how to adjust and how to live well with this chronic health issue. The tone of the conversation was serious and went on for nearly an hour. For the first time with me, Dad laid down the role of boss.

When I got off the phone my wife asked what had just happened. She could tell by my tone that something unusual had taken place in Missouri. Before I explained Dad's health discovery I gave her the generational report: "I just became the parent of my parent." With my ongoing relationship to my collegian children and a new connection to my dad, I was officially a member of the sandwich generation. For the first time I could feel the weight of trying to hold up both ends of the seesaw.

When Dad was beginning his final struggle with failing health I went to Missouri one January to check on my parents and to lead a conference. Dad was always a stickler about time. So the night before I headed west he called to double-check my arrival time. I reconfirmed my schedule. Then he said something that stuck in my ears: "While you're here, I want to go to the old farm one last time."

"One last time" . . . that phrase echoed in my imagination all the way to Missouri. So Mom, Dad, and I drove the 75 miles to the farm on Indian Creek early one morning. When we were within 15 miles or so of the old homestead a magical process happened: My parents became young again. As landmarks appeared through the car's windows they chattered about people, events, and memories. Half of their conversation began with "Remember when . . . " I knew I was on holy ground. I just listened with both ears and asked an occasional clarifying question. For about six hours we were suspended in a time capsule of rich memories.

On my visits to see my aging parents I always took a "research question" to ask them when the moment was right. After we got back from our visit to the old farm Dad and I were alone. He was in a mood to remember, so I asked my research question: "What was it like to grow up as one of the older children in a family of 12 kids?" Dad said that as soon as another child was born, Grandma switched her attention to the new arrival and farmed the younger kids out to the older children to care for. Then he began to cry and said about his mother, "I never sat on her lap. She never told me she loved me."

For the first time I saw the origin of my dad's parenting style and could finally cut him some slack. His parenting default setting was "not good enough!" Dad had championed education for me but hadn't attended my graduations. He'd prayed me into the ministry but could never inquire about my work. As a kid Dad hadn't been affirmed. So, supportiveness simply wasn't in his DNA. This discovery made me want to be even more outwardly supportive of my own children's life and work.

Some adults don't "make their move" in life until their late 50s.[4] Their early progress may have been interrupted and postponed by childrearing or by health crises or by detours from various causes. Having cleared those barriers, they can now bloom out and advance. For these special cases their risks are acts of faith.

Seizing Our 60s

The United States is experiencing a silver tsunami. Aging is in. For the first time in human history six generations are alive simultaneously. Our over-65 population is increasing by roughly 15 percent each decade. Watching our older neighbors, we see bucket lists being lived out, bodies slowing, women outliving men, and spirituality and gratitude becoming more natural. In response, services for older adults are mushrooming. Older adults now have specialized companies to help in preserving our "treasures" and memories, downsizing, and moving. Companion care and medical care online are plentiful resources. Our sixth decade is full of both unique opportunities and new turning points.

Adulthood spans three major turning points: entering young adulthood, navigating midlife, and transitioning to retirement. Of the three, retirement is often the most difficult to "get right," since there's less time for "do overs." Maturity is the key. Successful aging and retirement depend more on the person you are rather than the job you're in or will soon give up.

Maturity is on full display in pre-retirement and retirement, processes in our sixth decade for many of us. Retirement actually involves multiple transitions, each with a different degree of difficulty:

☐ Our **financial transition** into retirement may be the easiest of the four to calculate, only because it boils down to dollars and cents. The prospect of living on a fixed income is a sobering prospect. Much of life's earlier financial flexibility is lost when we move into retirement.

☐ Our **vocational transition** means laying aside the structures of jobs and finding meaning in other interests. Increasingly, retirement glides into encore careers or "re-hirement," as employment and volunteer work offer meaning without so much stress and pressure.

☐ Our **relational transition** may alter how we relate to family and friends. Casey Stengel, the well-known baseball player and manager from 1912 to 1965, retired home to California after a lifetime on the road. After a few weeks his wife announced that they had a breakfast and dinner marriage—not a breakfast, lunch, and dinner relationship. So Casey, who never met a stranger, became a greeter at his bank and spent his lunch breaks in the workplace for the decade until he died. Retirees often discover that those extra meals and that constant time together have to be negotiated.

☐ Our **emotional transition** into retirement is probably the most difficult for us, because it's most often left to last or ignored entirely. We miss our "place" in the world, our familiar routine, and the contributions we can make. We are forced to find our meaning in new ways. In truth, this psychological turning point should be mastered in the glide path prior to retirement rather than crashing and burning in the days after we pick up our gold watch.

In addition to multiple transitions our sixth decade confronts us with issues related to time management, aging, loss, and legacy.

How am I managing timelines and deadlines?

Moving through our 60s feels like a deadline decade with time as a precious commodity. It's a sobering decade and calls for soul-searching and planning.

When I turned 60 I could feel the weight of the deadlines looming on the horizon, so I enlisted a coach to help me identify how I'd spend "the second half of my life." We talked about the people and processes I value most. We looked for ways to stay engaged with those important people and processes. Three investments stood out and called for planned pursuit.

1. **Connections** to my adult children, my friends, and my mentees: These were long-term commitments, and I wanted to enrich these relationships every way I could.
2. **Creativity** through writing and teaching: I felt the lessons it had taken a lifetime to learn needed to be passed along.
3. **Coaching** others in their lives and ministries: I finished certification as a leader coach so I could continue to contribute to the growth of and futures of others.

How am I dealing with aging, as through the eyes of others?

We have a way of staying young in our own eyes, but we usually have a series of awakenings when we discover that others see us as older. Have you had any of the following experiences?

- ☐ **You receive a senior discount.** I was given a senior drink discount in the drive-through at McDonald's one morning. You know you're aging when people merely hear your voice and decide you're ancient!

- ☐ **Someone calls you "ma'am" or "sir" for the first time.** In that moment it's like being knighted with the solemn recognition, "I dub thee old."

- ☐ **You become invisible to some people in some places.** The author James Baldwin reported that he knew he was seen as a non-person as a black man when others looked through him and not at him. I know the feeling. In my mid-60s when I was in a problem-solving meeting at work and offered a possible solution, the group responded as if I hadn't even spoken. Over dinner that night I announced to my wife that I was officially seen as old in my own workplace.

- ☐ **People don't take the time to disagree with you.** When younger folks just smile and nod at your ideas or opinions, they may think you're old and irrelevant. In my late 20s I worked with Jim Slatton on a church staff in Dallas. I watched Jim, a world-class debater, relate to some of our older members by gently arguing with them. I asked why he pushed back in those cases. Jim pointed out that we discount our elders and patronize them when we don't consider them and their views important enough to test. It was an indelible lesson for a younger minister to learn then and for an older minister to live now.

Whose shoulders have I been standing on?

At age 69 I became an orphan when my mother, my last surviving parent, died. Listening to my parents during the final years of each of their lives clarified my understandings. Emotional legacy—what my parents and grand-parents had bequeathed to me—became more visible to me than ever before.

In a "Roots" moment I clearly sorted out their influences on me. I finally saw who had been holding the "cue cards" I'd read out loud all my life without recognizing the sources.

I was in Missouri with my ailing mother on Father's Day, 2009. I had been reflecting on how my parents, grandparents, and the only great-grandparent I'd known had lived. These seven elders, living more than 90 years on average, had each had direct access to me. And, each had left their direct imprints on me. Sorting out my elders' distinctive messages, I wrote a Father's Day note to my children and identified the lessons on each cue card.

- **"Stay free."—Great-grandma G:** My great-grandmother, a relative of Jesse James, had been widowed early, married an abusive second husband, "persuaded" him to leave home permanently (with the aid of a 54.40 buffalo rifle), and then raised two daughters alone. Freedom was not negotiable to her.

- **"Be curious."—Grandma D:** My paternal grandmother loved to read. She was the first person I knew who had a subscription to a news magazine. *Life*, with its oversized black-and-white photographs, delivered the globe to her mailbox every week. I wrote her a note on her 100th birthday and thanked her for giving me the curiosity to explore larger worlds beyond the Ozark Mountains.

- **"Heal your heart."—Grandpa D:** My grandfather may have died of a broken heart. He had 12 children, but the golden child, my uncle Loren, died in WWII when the *USS Asheville* sank in the South China Sea. Losing the son of promise created a gap in the family, but it left an open wound in Grandpa's heart. Every time Loren's name was mentioned for the quarter century or so Grandpa lived after the Great War, he would burst into uncontrollable sobs. It was like that grief stayed lodged in his throat, ready to gush out spontaneously. As a result, I've tried to deal with my losses directly and promptly.

- **"Go to school."—Dad:** My dad dropped out of high school during the Depression to help Grandpa support his large and growing family. That personal sacrifice made education highly valued to Dad and my family. When Dad joined the Army Air Corps in WWII, we sold our dairy herd. But, we kept two heifer calves to finance college educations for me and my four-month-old brother. I always knew I was destined to go to the university. Later, I got my PhD about the same time Dad earned his GED. He was probably prouder of his diploma than of my degree. So was I. A dream deferred had finally come true for him. I learned that life's key goals are worth waiting for.

☐ **"Maintain your independence."—Mom:** My mother left her remote southwestern Kansas home for a boarding high school and, at that young age, took responsibility for her life. She married, took charge of our household, and set the tone in every accounting job she held. While devoted to my dad, she always had her own sense of direction. She lived independently and still drove her car until shortly before her death at age 91. After she was gone we discovered she had some investments that only she knew about. Independent to the end, Mom showed me how to cultivate and keep my own voice.

☐ **"Read your Bible."—Grandma K:** My maternal grandmother was a no-nonsense, take-no-prisoners Midwestern woman. She was also extremely pious. I watched her teach an adult Bible class of men and women in her rural Baptist church and noted that no one challenged her interpretations. Later, I remember agreeing with her in discussions about the Bible even when I knew she was misinformed. With Grandma, you chose your battles cautiously, especially on matters of faith. She might be wrong occasionally, but she was rarely in doubt. Her example still reminds me to tread lightly around others' convictions.

☐ **"Life is play." —Grandpa K:** My mom, infant brother, and I lived with the Ks while Dad was in the military. At that time I was four years old; Grandpa K was 62 and endlessly fascinating to me. He'd been a real Virginia miner, Oklahoma cowboy, and Kansas homesteader. Grandpa played the banjo for me, taught me to rope, played catch with me, and let me shadow him around the farm. He was more fun than any "big person" I knew. The Depression and Dust Bowl had ended his successful farming operation and forced him to start life over from scratch at age 57. But he was always optimistic. His upbeat attitude remains an inspiration to me to this day.

All my life, like reading cue cards, I've heard myself almost automatically endorsing freedom and independence, curiosity and education, faith and fun. I can still see those distinctive cue cards in the near-dark just off-stage.

Knowing what "cue card" message each of these seven forebears held in my line of sight for me to "read" was new. I realize I clearly mirror their messages and amplify their values with my life and voice. I now see their distinct legacies and am grateful for their shoulders to stand on.

The Consultant's Loom

Bob, this is the portion of the journey I am now navigating, and so this chapter speaks deeply to me. The legacy questions that bubble up for me are often as troubling as they are welcome. Many days I find myself doing the hard work of discernment around whether the way I am spending my time aligns with the things I have said matter most. Far too often the patterns and schedules that dominate my calendar are there out of habit or to please others, rather than to provide an answer to the legacy questions. As I listen to colleagues and friends in this stage of life, I hear similar concerns.

A few years ago, Gordon McDonald wrote a book that meant a lot of me on living a resilient life.[5] Living a resilient life means being able to say "no" to lesser things so that you can say "yes" to higher things. For some, this involves a change of vocation or scenery. For most of us, however, it means we must engage in a thoughtful examination of why we are in the place (figuratively and literally) that we find ourselves. I have come through this journey with an unshakable conviction that I am now doing what God has been preparing me to do for many years.

Twenty-five years ago Bob Dale invited me to do a series of training events that started me down a path toward consultation and facilitation. Following that faint sense of call eventually led me to a series of events, relationships, and reading that gradually helped me see a great truth that I first read in McDonald's book. His contention is that the first half of our life is preparation for "the main event" that can only happen in the second half of our life. When I read that for the first time, it was like a shock of electricity ran through me. This author had been reading my mail! While fully engaged and thoroughly enjoying my life as a local church pastor, I increasingly sensed an attraction toward Christ's larger church and the very real issues it faces in the 21st century.

When I honestly pondered the idea that everything that happens before age 50 is preparation for the main event that is to come, I felt a depth of resonance and realization that I had never before known. Seeing this season of life (50s and 60s) as primetime and not decline was a true revelation to me. Doing so freed me up to pursue my sense of passion and call, and the deep needs I saw around me. Using the best counsel of Parker Palmer and Frederick Buechner, I listened to my life and allowed my dreams and desires to mesh with a sense of call to a church in desperate need. My resulting sense of call was so strong and magnetic that the reality of financial risk and downward mobility seemed a small price to pay for being in the center of God's dream for my life.

The resulting years of ministry have proven to be more meaningful than I had hoped for. I now find myself vitally engaged in ministry in a way that is both humbling and inspiring. Seeing God at work up-close in the lives of clergy and hundreds of congregations is at once challenging and invigorating. I can only give thanks that I have an opportunity in this season of my life to make a small contribution to the larger work of the Kingdom. My prayer for everyone in this season of life is a depth of call, joy, and satisfaction that defies description.

Many of the clergy I know best and talk with most are in this same season of discernment and discovery. Doing this work in the midst of a friendship or coaching relationship is one of the most energizing things I have had the pleasure of doing. I hope the readers of this book will take us up on our offer to help along that path of discovery!

Our Living-and-Giving Decades

Our fifth and sixth decades are platforms for mastering living-and-giving, the visible elements of our legacy. We would do well to ask ourselves:

- ☐ How have I matured as a leader and person of faith?
- ☐ How generous am I as a Christian?
- ☐ How effective am I as a parent of adult children?
- ☐ Is my faith growing, vibrant, and maturing?
- ☐ How are my personal involvements expanding in church and in service organizations?
- ☐ How am I reaching out beyond my own circles to the broader world?
- ☐ How am I planning for your future?

Our 50s and 60s focus on what matters most to us. Legacy and contribution issues dominate our lives and have been woven into the fabric now.

As leaders we long for "well done's" from God, our peers, and those who are waiting in the wings for their chance to make a difference. We're using the challenges we've mastered and are managing the mountains we still have to climb. But the journey isn't over. There's more weaving to do. What's ahead next?

Notes

[1] Daniel Levinson, *The Seasons of a Man's Life* (New York: Knopf, 1978), 275.

[2] Barbara Bradley Hagerty, *Life Reimagined: The Science, Art, and Opportunity of Midlife* (New York: Penguin, 2016).

[3] Frederick M. Hudson, *The Adult Years: Mastering the Art of Self-Renewal* (San Francisco: Jossey-Bass, 1991), 165-166.

[4] Ibid., 167.

[5] Gordon McDonald, *A Resilient Life: You Can Move Ahead No Matter What* (Nashville: Thomas Nelson, 2006).

"Wisdom" Threads
Leader Maturity for 70s and Older

Our 70s and beyond are decades for harvesting and sowing again. We can now reap the wisdom of maturing lives. In these older caring-and-sharing decades we have more to offer but less time to give away what we have. The African proverb's reminder is prophetic: "When an old person dies, a library burns down." Hard-won maturity reminds us that . . .

- ☐ We don't know everything.
- ☐ Having "thin skin" and taking offense are wastes of time.
- ☐ Only we are in charge of our behaviors.
- ☐ Listening teaches more than talking.
- ☐ We have a lot to laugh about, beginning with our own behaviors.
- ☐ A word of encouragement can turn lives around.
- ☐ Doing the right thing never goes out of style.

Maturity ripens into physical, emotional, and spiritual harvests for older people. Lots of older people are rapidly checking items off their "bucket lists," those things they still intend to do. In contrast, our wisest elders have "ribbon lists" of treasures and time they intend to wrap up and give away. Since wisdom travels light, elders are poised to give generously to the future of others. But along with the positive changes associated with aging, we face our share of challenges.

Challenges of Aging

When our age number begins with a seven, eight, nine, or another one, life fills up with challenges. New limits on health and energy settle into our lives. Financial concerns raise their ugly heads ahead of us. In the face of deadlines, time becomes even more precious to us. Relationships narrow as people we love are aging and dying too. Our clocks and calendars march on relentlessly. Just when we finally "have it all together," it takes more effort to remember where we put it. Thankfully, blessings accumulate alongside our burdens.

Paradoxically, we become "more like ourselves" as we age. Some of our civilized veneer wears off, and whatever has been lurking in the wings now walks to center stage. If we've always been in a rush, we may ease up on the accelerator. If we've been a fashion icon, we may make every day a casual Friday. If we've kept the lid on our temper, it may explode. If we've been mannerly and easy to please, we may now demand more time and attention from others. Aging has a way of letting the persons we really are break out of their safe places and storm the ramparts.

But elders don't let ourselves get run over so easily. We push back against Father Time. We try to extend our lives by keeping our bodies active and moving. We try to heal our hearts after "ouch" experiences by forgiving and by taking a longer view of life. We try to cultivate our souls by modeling hope through a grace-full lifestyle and a hope-full death-style. And, like Moses' father-in-law, Jethro, we offer perspective and guidance to younger generations (Exod. 18:1-27).

70-Something Perspectives

Our 70s may hear God's call to new challenges, like Abram who was called to risk the adventure of finding land, ancestry, and blessing as an older leader (Gen. 12:4). After six decades of experiences we, too, view life's possibilities uniquely:

☐ We see life from a perch that's closer to the end than the beginning or middle.

☐ We invest more in our highest values of faith, relationships, and contributions.

☐ We appreciate emotional and spiritual maturity.

☐ We now really believe what we believe.

☐ We preserve our lives for others with memories to savor and mementos to see and touch.

☐ We survey death with open eyes and prepare for our eventual end in practical, deliberate, and hopeful ways:
  • We steward our assets and legacies by making wills, naming executors, and assigning powers of attorney.
  • We clarify medical directives and arrange for organ donations.
  • We plan for the final celebrations of our lives, specifying our preferences for funerals and burials or cremations.
  • We expect our family circles to rebalance and reassign leader roles naturally after funerals, just as family equilibrium adjusts after weddings, births, and divorces.

The way we die is often a testimony to the way we lived, isn't it? My mother died in a care facility just short of her 92nd birthday. After recovering from breaking her back in a one-car accident, she developed congestive heart failure and steadily declined over six months. My wife and I went to Springfield, Missouri, to help care for her. After we arrived at her bedside she waited until we left her room for lunch, and then she died during a prayer with the chaplain. As an ever-independent person, she even chose her time and manner of death.

The way the care facility dealt with death was also a statement of faith. The chaplain invited the family to Mom's bedside to say our good-byes. Then, the family left the room so the body could be bathed and readied for transport to the mortuary. The family was then invited back into the room to accompany the body out of the building.

The elder care facility had a simple practice. The employees brought every patient in the front door and took each body back out that same door. The walk from the death room to the front door was almost like a worship service or military parade, with staff and visitors standing respectfully as the body was wheeled past. After the body was transported to be prepared for burial, the death room was cleaned and left vacant for a week.

Our preferences can become plans, testifying to hope and freedom. May it be so for us.

We turn life into our own research project and continue to learn as we go. We may be growing older, but the adventure isn't over. Satchel Paige, the pioneering black baseball pitcher who was blocked from the major leagues by segregation, asked a telling question: "How old would you be if you didn't know how old you are?"

Events in Our 80s and 90s

Today's elders, in our 80s and 90s or even approaching 100 like Abram and Sarah (Gen. 21:1-7), are still creating new frontiers for all who follow:

- For the first time in human history we have enough people in their 80s and beyond to do studies of a new late-life stage.
- Multi-generational interactions are now more frequent and more meaningful.
- New attention is being given to studying our "super-agers," those special folks whose brains are much younger and nimbler than their age peers.

- ☐ Telemedicine, electronic monitors, and home health care robots are beginning to provide residential care assistance.
- ☐ Communal housing options for elders are springing up, creating second-chance families in shared settings.
- ☐ American universities are providing near-campus housing developments for alumni and other elders, including class audits and culture-rich experiences.
- ☐ Elderhood is becoming an extension of middle life.
- ☐ "Being" is balanced with "doing."

Those of us who are 70 and older live in a distinctive moment in history. As a growing segment of the population, we are more visible and important than the aging generations that have preceded us.

Wisdom's Spiritual Equity

Younger generations have steadily invested sweat equity in themselves. Now, elder generations can and do strategically invest spiritual equity—maturity's inner growth from lives well lived—in others' futures.

Wisdom, our enriched perspective from experience, is God's gift to us. Sages, a select group of people with "heavenly horse-sense," are featured in the Bible's "wisdom literature."[1] As Proverbs 1:7 notes, these practical tutor-guides stand in awe of God, are made wise by him, and pass their wisdom along to younger generations. In Scripture the sages taught younger leaders—mostly royals—to make good, prudent, godly choices.[2] The examples of the sages and elders who presided over decisions at the village gates have set the stage for contemporary sharers of wisdom. Those sages reinvested their spiritual equity, and so can we.

In today's world some religious traditions are reviving an old movement: blessing their elders to transform aging into "sage-ing."[3] Faith elders are stepping forward to encourage and guide younger generations. Older community members who understand life deeply and broadly are precious resources for emerging leaders. These sage leaders provide practical functions to their communities:

- ☐ **Sage leaders tell the community's stories.** They identify origins, interpret turning points, and tell hope stories. They're walking history books, sharing tales of identity and redemption, births and deaths, marriages and family feuds, conflicts and reconciliations.

Wise sages remind communities who they are, where they are, where they're going, and how they have arrived at hinges of history.

☐ **Sage leaders are truth tellers.** As living consciences and moral compasses for their community, the wise people point to spiritual advance. Discernment is a basic gift sages give to their communities.

Discerning our truth has its own timetable. Years later I now see my education in a different light. Seminary and graduate studies gave me a solid theological, biblical, and historical footing. But congregational leadership is mostly learned on the run and from stubbing your toes. While you're dusting yourself off, you size up what just happened, note some lessons, and promise yourself that you'll never go down that road again. Then, fortified with new discoveries, you move ahead with more confidence (and make some brand-new mistakes).

Looking back, I realize I learned much more about human nature while managing apartment houses during seminary than in the hallowed classrooms on The Hill. I managed one house with four apartments, and not one single family moved from that house intact during the years I oversaw the property. Each family dissolved in its own way. Each taught me something new. While mopping, painting, and cleaning up after they'd left, I thought about their unique crises and tried to make sense of the problems we humans create for ourselves.

One day the police arrived at the jinxed house with flashing lights and fanfare. I hurried across the street to the house to see what the fuss was about. A woman resident had taken too many pain pills, had fallen off the front porch onto the lawn, and had made a dazed decision that her alcoholic husband had beaten her up. The husband was arrested, but then cleared when the investigation was completed.

In a follow-up conversation that couple invited me to attend an AA meeting with them. Given my background, I was in a world I knew nothing about. Addictions, I learned, vary from person to person. I even found two pieces of myself in those AA meetings.

First, unlike my hosts, I found I was an acceptable, even an admired, addict. My workaholism was already moving me up the career ladder. Ironically, it would also break my health later.

Second, I discovered why certain flaws made me so angry. They were my own flaws, reflected into my eyes from others' behaviors, and therefore visceral threats to me.[4] I learned those two lessons in an apartment building on Eighth Avenue in Fort Worth, Texas. I now recognize that building as one of my most important schoolhouses.

☐ **Sage leaders mediate community disagreements.** Peacemakers bridge community chasms and reconcile factions. The sage's ability to see the big picture helps others see beyond their individual interests, glimpse others' viewpoints, and consider the well-being of the larger community.

I once consulted with a church in conflict. Unfortunately, it wasn't new territory for those folks. They'd fought long and well, already firing a previous consultant. When I arrived they were mad at everyone; I was just a new enemy. I saw quickly that I wouldn't be able to resolve their problems, so I admitted my ineffectiveness to them. Then I asked if they'd consider naming the 10 more trusted members of the church and letting them lead the peacemaking efforts. To my surprise, the church agreed. Probably to everyone's surprise, the trusted 10 guided the entire church into a reconciliation process that was deeply healing. The sages were put in charge of the church's health and ministry. That decision made all the difference for the future.

☐ **Sage leaders model the link between past and future.** They personally bridge generations and eras. Sages live out loud. They openly demonstrate integrity, die with serenity, and live on in community memories and stories.

Lives Well Lived, Futures Still Open

As we pass the threshold of three score and ten, we begin to appreciate what's meant by having "old souls." We become stewards of the wisdom of years. What are the growth questions that measure the wisdom of elders? Consider the following:

How have I maintained child-like curiosity?

Jesus instructed those who seek God's kingdom to adopt the mind of a child (Matt. 18:2). As Christian disciples we're life-long growers, always rookies at heart. We cultivate wonder and look for frontiers. When the famed cellist, Pablo Casals, was asked why he continued to practice his instrument at age

90, he replied, "Because I think I'm making progress." That's a child's attitude and spirit.

At age 71 I discovered I had cancer. My cancer was usually a slow-growing and very treatable family of cancers. Although the "C word" is scary to hear when it's applied to you, I wasn't overly worried. A work friend had survived more than 20 years with my type of cancer.

Then, additional tests showed my cancer was an extremely dangerous, unusually fast-growing type. The cancer had to be removed as soon as possible. A church friend had had a similar surgery and found his recovery had been made easier by robotic procedures. So, after some consultation, I chose to have robotic surgery too.

The good news is that my cancer is gone. My doctors and I monitor my health and check for cancer every 90 days, and I've remained cancer-free as I near the fourth year after surgery.

As a cancer survivor I've learned a lot about myself. I was almost an outside observer of my own disease and healing process. Additionally, it's been interesting to step inside others' pilgrimage with the "C word" disease and to walk with them. The most helpful outcome to me is how I can now serve as a guide and sounding board for others who are dealing with cancer. Curiosity about health crises leads to some hard-won wisdom.

How have I viewed and understood the unfolding of history?

More than simply seeing lots of years, wise people have connected the dots and placed lives into a larger frame. Wisdom values continuity and calling.[5] Continuity, the ability to see that the chapters of our lives are firmly connected, connects dots and keeps us moving ahead smoothly. Calling, the sense that God has plans for our lives that we can fulfill easily, provides wider frameworks of meaning and don't fade with age. Continuity and calling interpret life's larger and longer themes.

As Ecclesiastes 3:1-6 wisely reminds us, timing is everything. For example, in most people's eyes "finishing well" is completed with retirement. For most, retirement marks the winding down of a life. Like sprinters, these workers run to the tape and quit. Bob Buford, in his book *Finishing Well*, extends the race. He tells of interviews he had with 60 leaders who ran through the tape and are living their later years on purpose. Buford describes these "code breakers"[6] as pioneers, pathfinders, and map makers for a new and largely unknown territory. These restless leaders see and pursue abundant opportunities for meaningful service in later years.

Buford's primary "wisdom figure" is Peter Drucker,[7] the late business and leadership consultant and author with more than four million words in print. Drucker stressed finding islands of health and strength as anchors for our lives. In Drucker's experience, inexperienced leaders can see only four years or so down the road. In contrast, experienced leaders have a time horizon of 20 or 30 years. That longer perspective invites "Life II" and its new chapters to be lived well.

Buford's interviews spotlight the search for meaning beyond midlife. Repositioning, or keeping your core values while changing how you apply them, is the key Buford found in living productively across retirement's threshold. Finishing well, according to Buford, is a matter of recognizing new life seasons and bridging over into these later seasons with purpose.

How have I used contexts as containers for meaning?

Contextual awareness emerges from an array of attention-grabbing experiences—faith, education, victories, travel, tragedies, understanding our era of history—and other elements that stretch our imaginations and widen our world. All of life becomes research materials for creating wider viewscapes and deeper perspectives.

In 1989 Charles Chandler and I started a professional support group that still meets regularly throughout the year and holds an annual overnight retreat. In the early meetings we included book reviews and personal sharing. We soon dropped the book discussions and now focus only on exploring our personal issues. In our nearly 30 years together we've faced deaths, severe illnesses, marital and family stressors, job losses, and faith challenges.

Like the deliberate flaw in Navajo weaving, I've noticed an almost mystical element in our support group's sessions. In every meeting one or two of us is in pain, and the rest of us are doing well. The ones of us who are whole that day gather around the one or two who are bent or broken to encourage, help find solutions, and pray. The roles change from meeting to meeting. At one time or another all of us have limped in wounded, and all of us have bandaged the others' wounds. Each of us knows that our wounds will have their turn. We rely on this band of brothers to stand and kneel with us.

The sweep of time and the variety of experiences that have occurred in my support group have helped me see and understand contexts. Part of wisdom is finding meaning amid life's twists and turns, and that discovery takes time. So many years of observing our group's personal and professional ebbs and flows have provided a tutorial in perspective.

How have I aged with optimism and a positive attitude?

We don't all "live happily ever after." Staying upbeat when life takes bumpy roads calls for cultivating a "glass half full" view of life. Bennis and Thomas describe this quality as "neoteny,"[8] an enduring sense of wonder and discovery. Elders with youthful, joyous, and adaptive lifestyles overcome obstacles. With this strong ability, elders can turn hardships into lifelong learning. Wonder has a way of transforming our burdens into blessings. But what if you've been labeled a loser?

You've probably never heard of William Henry Brisbane.[9] But in the 1840s he ran an apothecary shop in Cincinnati, after failing as a farmer, publisher, and physician. William had inherited a sizeable fortune of $100,000 and burned through it quickly. Consequently, he was denied a loan because the credit agency of his era judged he'd remain a failure for the rest of his life.

But there was another side to William's story. He had earlier owned and operated a successful South Carolina plantation. William decided slavery was wrong. He sold out and moved to the North. He felt guilty that he'd left his slaves behind, though, so William spent his $100,000 inheritance to buy them back and set them free.

William Henry Brisbane wasn't a loser after all. Although his life was judged in the win-lose cultural context of the Civil War and Industrial Revolution, William found ways to see possibilities and contribute positively to the lives of others. He redeemed his life and the futures of others.

Paying It Forward—and Backward

So what can elders do for younger generations now? How can caring and sharing proceed? Consider these ways:

- ☐ We can pray from the sidelines for their discernment, courage, strength, and futures.
- ☐ We can walk beside them as extra eyes, ears, and hearts to add to their senses of situations and opportunities.
- ☐ We can help them craft and improve their lives.

My parents were both crafters. My dad was a carpenter. It was instructive to help him "true up" walls and floors, making them straight, level, and plumb. I still have his old framing square to remind me to stay "true." My mom was a quilter and gave quilts as gifts at births and marriages. She used a variety of materials to make her quilt blocks and then combine them into classic patterns. I have several of her quilts to remind me that beauty and utility can be joined. My parents' crafting examples guide me and help me guide others.

Like Navajo weavers, we can coach strength and beauty. And, as leaders, we can face flaws in ourselves and others. We can actively coach the NOW, NEW, and NEXT leaders in their places of service. And, that brings us to the challenge of pooling and clustering mature leaders for greater impact and service.

A few years back I consulted with members of an international ministry group about a new leader development program they were designing. They needed an approach that spanned cultures, generations, and technologies. One of their staffers wondered out loud where they'd find leaders old enough to understand these challenges. It's natural and correct to look for experienced leaders, but it was the wrong question.

My question in response ran against the grain. I asked, "Where can you find leaders young enough to understand these challenges?" In some situations the wisdom of youth trumps the wisdom of age. When ministry approaches to different cultures, emerging generations, and new technologies are in the balance, think young. For these particular kinds of challenges, younger leaders may actually have more understanding than older ones.

It was interesting to watch the internal conflict this tension triggered in the ministry group. In the end these leaders couldn't overcome their bias in favor of age. By facing their future traditionally, these leaders limited the very resource they were creating.

Actually, the best solution to new and novel problems is often co-mentoring across generations. Many of us have been tutored in technologies by younger folks who have grown up with changing technologies. In these cases younger generations are comfortable with issues older generations haven't encountered as directly. The balance of old-to-young and young-to-old perspectives in teams creates lots of solution-finding firepower and leaves fewer blind spots.

The Consultant's Loom

Bob, this is the world you live in and know well. Like you, at every step of my journey, I have been blessed by people in this stage of life who have invested in me and taught me invaluable lessons.

I think of your influence across the years and the way you have deliberately tried to call out gifts and talents of younger clergy and leaders. What an immeasurable gift you have given a host of us.

Early on I was blessed to be taught some hard lessons in humility. I went from being a "know-it-all" at 30 to being afraid I knew absolutely nothing at 35. People like you helped me recover from my hubris and find the way of humility as I fumbled my way into the future. As I think about those people in their 70s and beyond who have blessed me along the journey, I could write a novel and never say enough about what they have taught me. Most are people who taught me without intending to. They simply lived life fully and trusted God completely. The result was an example I could depend upon when life got difficult or challenging for me. A sampler would include:

- From Robert and Jean Woody I learned the value of Bible study, prayer, and life-long learning.
- From Don and Trudy Rose I learned about humor and the ability to handle the hard things of life.
- From Robert and Elsie Burger I learned wisdom and commonsense.
- From Rose Ingram I learned about beauty and nature.
- From Stu Crow, Dan Stubbs, and Walt Hendrix I learned how to be organized and think logically.
- From Jess and June Noell I learned about patience and honesty.
- From Charles and Betty Langford I learned about loyalty.
- From Carl Griggs, Stella Boyles, Gene Kirk, Leta Faye Roberts, Jim Reich, John Tice, Sherwood Jones and Jack Turner I learned what is most valuable.
- From Billy Nimmons, Charlie Bowen, Mark Pace, and a host of others I learned how to enjoy life and treasure each day fully.
- From Reggie McDonough, Bob Dale, Buddy Shurden, Larry McSwain, and George Bullard I learned to never stop learning.

The list of my teachers would fill a library, for I have been fortunate to be surrounded by older adults who lived a life of faith and cared deeply for those who came behind them. I can only hope and pray that God will allow me to occupy that role in the lives of others.

From "What?" to "So What?"

Now we move from "what" to "so what." We've woven the strong threads of theology together with the texture threads of maturity. That's the "what" for faithful leaders—mystery and maturity. In the "so what" exploration we'll see how this mystery-maturity tapestry is put together in congregational leader-ship teams. Ready?

Let's complete the weaving now, creating collaborative teams with breadth and balance.[10] Let's explore ways that clusters of strong and mature leaders with complementary gifts can accomplish more together than singly.

Notes

[1] The Bible's wisdom literature is characterized by the practical advice in Proverbs, Ecclesiastes, Song of Solomon, Job, some Psalms, and some instructional passages in the New Testament.

[2] Gordon D. Fee and Douglas Stuart, *How to Read the Bible for All It's Worth: A Guide to Understanding the Bible*, 2nd ed. (Grand Rapids: Zondervan, 1993), 206-230.

[3] Zalman Schachter-Shalomi and Ronald S. Miller, *From Age-ing to Sage-ing: A Profound New Vision of Growing Older* (New York: Warner Books, 1995). Also see, Sharon Wegscheider-Cruse, *Becoming a Sage: Discovering Life's Lessons One Story at a Time* (Deerfield Beach, FL: Health Communications, Inc., 2016).

[4] Mark I. Rosen, *Thank You for Being Such a Pain: Spiritual Guidance for Dealing with Difficult People* (New York: Harmony Books, 1998).

[5] Bob Buford, *Finishing Well: What People Who REALLY Live Do Differently!* (Nashville: Integrity Publishers, 2004), 146-147.

[6] Ibid., xvi.

[7] Bruce Rosenstein, *Living in More Than One World: How Peter Drucker's Wisdom Can Inspire and Transform Your Life* (San Francisco: Berrett-Koehler Publishers, 2009).

[8] Warren G. Bennis and Robert J. Thomas, *Geeks and Geezers: How Era, Values, and Defining Moments Shape Leaders* (Boston: Harvard Business School Press, 2002).

[9] Scott A. Sandage, *Born Losers: A History of Failure in America* (Boston: Harvard Business School Press, 2005).

[10] David A. Hennan and Warren Bennis, *Co-Leaders: The Power of Great Partnerships* (New York: Wiley, 1999).

PART 3

Weaving Leader Teams
Growing Down, Growing Up, Growing Together

Welcome to our final "grow down, grow up" challenge: the team tapestry. When we've grown down and up, then we're better able to grow together.

We've "woven" individual leaders with threads of theology and maturity, but we aren't finished yet. Let's create teams or clusters of leaders who can blend together effectively and balance each other's strengths and blind spots. Let's weave ministry teams that can combine inside health with outside reach.

It's time to make a tapestry of rich leadership roles. Let's look at a leader team model and then weave you in. Ask yourself:

- [ ] What's my best ministry contribution to a tapestry of teamwork?
- [ ] How do I fit into the team's tapestry?
- [ ] Where do I still need to grow?
- [ ] Am I a NOW, NEW, NEXT, or NEAR leader?

NOW, NEW, NEXT, and NEAR

Blending Leader Strengths

The weaving process is nearly complete. Leaders grow down, deepened by theology and faith. Leaders grow up, heightened by maturity and life experience. Taken together, a leadership tapestry is almost ready to be put on display.

But we're still on the loom. Our inner lives are now primed to be lived outwardly—practicing, relating, and mobilizing. What would it look like if we deliberately wove together leader teams with different levels of experience, various gifts, and distinctive roles? Let's grow together.

Weaving Teams on the Leadership Loom

Something mystical happens when ministry teams gel and work well. Our personal stories then morph into team stories. We join a team pilgrimage toward a team destiny.

God's natural order illustrates teamwork (Matt. 13:24-30, 47-50). For example, redwood trees are so massive their root systems can't hold these huge trees upright during severe storms. How have redwoods survived for centuries? They "hold hands." They interlock their root systems underground and hold each other up. They form a living, growing, steadying community that lasts. That's how effective ministry teams function too. We support each other.

When faith is woven together, no longer are we mere individuals, no longer women and men, no longer young or old. Differences now enrich our common work. Our larger calling from Christ becomes our core story that bonds, builds, and blesses us as a team. Our different roles on the team blend into deeper ways to relate and better ways to magnify each other's gifts. We may be the stars of our personal stories, but as ministry partners we all have parts and places in the shared redemptive spotlight.

- ☐ How do we complement each other?
- ☐ How do we create clusters of leaders that leave no blind spots?
- ☐ How do we share theology?
- ☐ How do we grow mature leaders with faith for each life stage and ministry challenge?

- [ ] How do we put mature leaders together in teams?
- [ ] How do we bless and empower those leaders to serve God's kingdom?
- [ ] How can we weave together a blend of NOW, NEW, NEXT, and NEAR leaders?
- [ ] How do these leader strengths mesh and work together?

The following team leadership model weaves together seasoned and emerging leaders, practicing and prepping leaders. The blend and balance are powerful elements, effective for congregations and communities. As you explore this model, think of your ministry teams.

GROWING LEADER CLUSTERS:
"NOW," "NEW," "NEXT," "NEAR" LEADERS

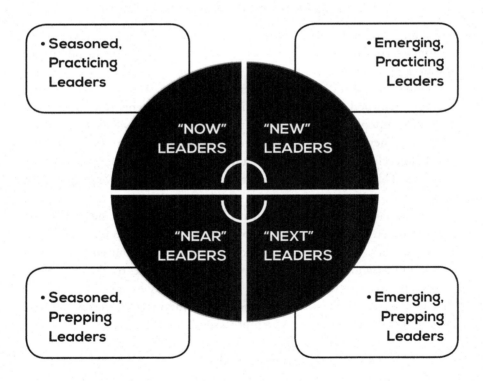

NOW Leaders:
Operating in the Hot Seat

NOW leaders operate from the first seat, the hot seat. Seasoned and practicing leaders, they stand at center stage, squarely in the cross-hairs. They live and lead in the "now." First in a team of equals, they're visible and responsible. NOW leaders fill leadership roles with no places to hide, places that are heady and humbling at the same time.

NOW leaders have two pivotal and high-profile responsibilities: advancing the community's calling and cultivating other leaders. NOW leaders set the pace in pursuing organizational goals—a basic in all leadership. They are often credited with the organization's success or failure, with progress or decline.

To advance the community's calling, the most effective NOW leaders surround themselves with a rich blend of balanced co-leaders. The mix of gifts, talents, and experiences adds strength to the leadership cluster. This mix minimizes blind spots, gaps, and weak areas as well.

NOW leaders grow other staff leaders with versatility, adaptability, and agility—the Swiss Army knives of religious and service communities. As staff leaders, NOW leaders develop NEW and NEXT leaders and may invite NEAR leaders into the teamwork. As Stephen Covey reminds us, "You have to water the flowers you want to grow."[1]

The Bible brims with NOW leaders—pacesetters who take the risks of responsibility. Jesus is the ultimate example of a NOW leader. Look at the simple actions he concentrated on: When he declared his public ministry he gathered a diverse team of 12 around him. For the emerging faith community he charged them with preaching and healing. For their own leadership development, he took them "with him." (See Mark 3:14.)

Moses was another NOW leader. He confronted Pharaoh, rallied the dispirited Hebrews, and heroically led the tribes out of Egypt toward the Promised Land. Over time he involved his siblings, Aaron and Miriam, in the leader team. His legacy as a NOW leader is unmistakable. It's no surprise that Moses is mentioned in the New Testament more than any other Old Testament leader.

In their teams NOW leaders function much like musical conductors. Like orchestra conductors they blend strengths, drawing what's needed by the team into the foreground, on time and in tune. Or, like leaders of jazz combos they set the baseline and give other leaders opportunities to step to the front of the stage and improvise around the team's theme.

NEW Leaders:
Moving into the Arena

NEW leaders join organizational leader teams in progress. They're moving into a new arena or place of leadership, but they aren't new to leadership. As emerging and practicing leaders, they fill key roles and take on major responsibilities. NEW leaders add experience, confidence, and perspective to the staff mix. Moving into a fresh ministry arena, they both welcome and provide supervision and mentoring. NEW leaders complement NOW leaders and other teammates in ministry.

Think of Paul's first congregational ministry with Barnabas in Antioch (Acts 11:19–13:3). In that setting Barnabas was the NOW leader, mentioned first in the ministry team with Paul as the NEW leader. Paul contributed to the work in Antioch while watching and learning. Soon he was ready to step into the NOW role and lead missionary outreach in the early church.

The Consultant's Loom

Upon graduation from seminary I was invited to join the ministerial team at a large church and continue my transition into the NEW phase of my ministry. There I found mentors and friends, both laity and clergy, who nurtured me and provided opportunities to grow and to learn what it meant to be an effective minister. Some of those lessons were exhilarating and some were excruciating, but all were valuable.

Challenges

From the lessons I learned during my early ministry and from my observations of many NEW leaders in the years since, I found that NEW leaders must cultivate an appreciation for and comfort with the following:

☐ **Uncertainty.** A substantial part of your job will fall under "other duties as assigned" tasks. You will often find yourself creating ministries and trying things you have no specific training for. That "chaordic" lifestyle is both friend and foe. It calls out the most creative part of you, but it also creates great stress and anxiety. How you manage the uncertainty in your vocational life will go far in determining your effectiveness and sense of satisfaction.

☐ **Being a student of others.** You will spend much time in a learning mode. Good students begin with an essential realization: you don't know all you need to know. Good ministers are hungry for knowledge. You understand that formal education is a prelude to the main event of learning. Cultivating an inquiring heart and mind is a prerequisite for effectiveness in ministry. That spirit continues in good leaders.

☐ **Being overlooked.** Sitting on the bench can be extremely frustrating. Ministry is humbling in multiple ways, one of which is realizing that the kingdom of God is going to be fine—with or without your contribution. Granted, we all want to do our part to enhance the church, but the humility of a healthy minister comes as we take ourselves less seriously. Early in ministry we often find ourselves out of the limelight as others with more experience and status blot out our efforts. That is actually a helpful awareness and life lesson, if we are wise enough to appropriate it.

☐ **Patience.** NEW clergy are often ready to practice ministry but not prepared to do the hard work of theological reflection, foundation-building, and relationship-building that precedes public ministry. Waiting our turn and absorbing truth at every opportunity requires great patience and emotional intelligence. NEW leaders are wise to cultivate such disciplines as learning from others as they experience ministry, debriefing them, waiting patiently for the opportunity, and then being ready when called upon.

☐ **Not having all the answers.** NEW leaders come onto the job with great enthusiasm and a head full of ministry ideas, theology, doctrine, ecclesiology, missiology, and worship expertise. Blending those insights with a sense of humility is a fine art. Acknowledging our ignorance as well as our insights is one of the great tasks of a NEW leader. Inviting trusted friends to keep you honest and humble will serve you well in this season of life and ministry.

Intentionality

NEW ministers must learn the necessity of intentionality. Being proactive rather than reactive will enable you to focus your life and ministry toward what you feel led to, rather than the things that are pushed upon you. To that end, NEW clergy leaders are wise to be deliberate about the following:

☐ **Learning.** Every week is a learning lab filled with potential insights.

☐ **Time management and discipline.** Ministerial leadership life is deceptive. What appears from a distance to be a simple, singular existence is actually one of the most demanding and multifaceted careers imaginable. Managing schedules and maintaining disciplined habits around self-care are learned and ingrained in the early years of the work. Remember, most clergy find that our ministry life escalates in complexity across the years. It seldom reverses course toward simplicity. Master these issues now, or pay a price for a lifetime.

☐ **Humility.** The role of NEW leader implies a degree of humility in the very name and concept. You are not yet fully vested as a leader. An accompanying sense of humility and vulnerability is a key predictor for future effectiveness in ministry. Cultivating this self-awareness now sets in motion invaluable emotionally intelligent habits and thought patterns.

☐ **Service.** Along with a humble spirit, a willingness to do "whatever it takes" is a great predictor of life-long success. Leadership, according to Jesus, is bottom-up rather than top-down. Nowhere else is this played out for congregational leaders in as prominent a way as when we exhibit a spirit of service first and being served second.

☐ **Cultivating emotional intelligence.** It took me 30 years into ministry to learn the language and theory of emotional intelligence (EQ). It immediately resonated with what I had seen and experienced across the years as a leader. Theory, facts, doctrine, and raw data do not necessarily persuade or encourage people. Understanding the power of EQ and learning to enhance our own EQ, along with working out of an emotionally intelligent model, is essential for congregational leaders.

☐ **Family.** Early experiences of balancing family and vocational demands establish valuable patterns and trajectories for congregational leaders. NEW leaders often find that issues tied to one's family of origin emerge in early ministry settings. Those issues have profound impacts on our immediate family and upon our functioning in a congregational family. Finding information, encouragement, therapy, and thoughtful colleagues to help you through those days of insight and challenge is paramount.

☐ **Boundaries.** NEW clergy will surely wrestle with the dilemmas of maintaining a strong sense of self and differentiating where professional and personal lines are drawn. The very best intentions are swept away in the realization that there is more to do in the job than could ever be accomplished in the time we have allotted. Along with the discipline of time management and self-care, boundary awareness is a life-long journey of thoughtfulness and consistency.

☐ **Devotional core.** Personal spiritual disciplines and habits are often established during the NEW season of ministry life. A devotional life serves as the enduring core through the ups and downs of congregational life. Failure to feed that core is at the heart of many cases of burn-out, brown-out, acting-out, and dropping-out of ministry. Conversely, maintaining consistent patterns of study, prayer, and solitude build a foundation that endures.

☐ **Choosing adaptive leadership models and methods.** One of the great gifts of recent research is Ron Heifetz' material on adaptive leadership.[2] When clergy learn to distinguish between technical challenges and adaptive challenges, much energy is saved for battles that merit the effort. NEW leaders who cultivate that insight establish lifetime patterns.

Contributions

NEW leaders are often brought into an established team of lay and clergy leaders who have history, patterns, and unspoken rules of operation. Finding a true seat at the table and a space for your voice is not as easy as just showing up for work. In such a setting a NEW leader must acknowledge the complexity of self-discovery occurring at the same time that assimilation into a leadership culture is underway. This delicate dance of leadership is compounded by the lives and drama of others around you, along with the unpredictable nature of ministry in a local church. This dance may involve:

☐ **Energy.** Early days of ministry can be times of heightened energy and capacity for work.

☐ **Passion.** NEW ministers often find a deep sense of passion for the work of God in the life of the church. Idealized expectations and romantic notions of changing the world can provide abundant fuel for ministry.

☐ **Inquisitiveness.** NEW leaders often bring a refreshing willingness to question standard practices and long-held traditions.

☐ **Questions.** Simply asking "Why?" in ministry settings can evoke intense reactions from a team.

☐ **Impatience.** Congregational life tends to move at "glacial pace." The resulting impatience and frustration, when properly managed, is a gift to a leadership culture that has grown complacent or stuck.

Needs

NEW leaders enter a leadership team or system with a wide range of needs. Some NEW leaders are self-aware enough to know this; others will, hopefully, learn about them. Either way, wise ministry teams are deliberate about addressing and engaging these needs. In doing so they help to cultivate these NEW leaders as they grow up, down, and out in their ministry.

☐ **Seasoning.** When NEW leaders are encouraged to experience a wide array of ministries and events, with an understanding that they are as much student as teacher, everyone benefits. Realistic expectations include an awareness that experience is a better teacher than the classroom. Healthy leadership teams provide NEW leaders opportunities for experiential learning.

☐ **Wisdom.** Imparting wisdom appropriately is a great gift from a team to a NEW leader. Learning how each person receives and benefits from wisdom transfer is more art than science, and strong teams pay attention to this.

☐ **Patience.** You would think this reality of life with a NEW leader goes without saying, but it is often the case that teams underestimate how much patience a NEW leader will require. Like children learning a new skill, it is substantial.

☐ **Understanding.** Established teams may have forgotten the emotional rollercoaster that entry into a leadership situation evokes. Empathic listening and assurances that tomorrow will come are part of the plan for helping NEW leaders survive the early days of ministry.

☐ **Encouragement.** NEW leaders will make mistakes and need a safe landing place when they fall and/or fail. Healthy leadership teams take seriously their role as guides and mentors along that journey.

Preparation

As a NEW leader you are preparing for a life or season of ministry. Being deliberate and thoughtful about this phase of your career allows you to wring as much meaning as possible out of the time you spend on a team and in a congregation. It would be beneficial to ask yourself certain questions:

☐ Why am I doing this?
☐ What are my goals?
☐ What will it look like if I am successful?
☐ Who am I trying to please?
☐ What's it like to work with me?

Think of the contrasts in NEW Leaders. A healthy NEW leader brings energy and enthusiasm to the group; is respectful of tenure, age, and experience; listens more than speaks; avoids triangles; cultivates a strong work ethic; challenges and resists when principles get trampled; and is humble and reflective about motives.

In contrast an unhealthy NEW leader feels entitled, lives an unexamined life, creates rivalries, cultivates followers, dismisses experience, gives up too easily, and is sloppy and unprofessional.

There was a moment in my NEW phase of ministry when I seriously considered leaving the ministry. Six years into my career I had experienced plenty of success, but also significant failures and disappointments. I had been a member of a congregational ministry team during a time of tremendous upheaval and discord. What had started out as a Camelot-like experience had descended into something approaching purgatory. For all of my love of the church and my sense of call to ministry, I was also confronted with the difficulties of working with imperfect people and the foibles of my own life.

At this critical juncture, things were especially difficult at work, and the alternative of a secular career that offered financial security and reasonable hours was increasingly attractive. I went so far as to schedule a meeting with a friend who had offered me a job in the financial services industry, if I wanted to pursue it.

Over the course of several days leading up to the meeting I sought out trusted staff teammates and advisors to help me think clearly. They asked hard questions and pressed me to delve more deeply than simply reacting to the pain I was experiencing. They pushed me to re-examine my call and to admit ways in which I had helped create the crisis through mismanaging time, family, boundaries, and a vibrant devotional life. They invited me to imagine a better tomorrow and to believe that God's promises were still in play for my life. Gradually that team helped me to see the possibilities I would be walking away from, and to see the potential in myself I had never fully appreciated.

I found an especially meaningful relationship with an older minister, a NEAR leader who would soon be retiring from active ministry. We were on opposite ends of the vocational timeline, but he took time with me and gave me extraordinary insight and wisdom. For hours at a time he quizzed, prodded, probed, and pressed me. He listened empathically and shared many of his own struggles. In the end he patiently allowed me to come to a clear and confident decision that settled the matter for the rest of my career.

I passed on the lucrative financial services career and reengaged in congregational ministry with newfound insights and wisdom. I had spent nearly 10 years at that point in secondary leadership roles, always getting ready to lead, and now began to turn my attention to opportunities to step more fully into the role of team leader/pastor. I was ready to step into the arena and put my preparation into practice as a NEW leader.

NEXT Leaders:
Learning the Ropes from the Bench

NEXT leaders have been identified either by others or have volunteered for service themselves,[2] and thus are being cultivated for future leadership. NEXT leaders are poised to move from the bench into the game. They are emerging leaders who are preparing for larger roles in ministry. They are making a difference already and will contribute much more as they learn the ropes fully.

NEXT leaders are prominent in the biblical record. Jesus prepared his followers and sent them into the harvest fields before they were fully "ripe." After his dramatic conversion Paul stepped back to sort out his calling and to discern his next steps. Moses, exiled to the backside of the desert, used that quiet time to grow up and down. Emerging leaders know they have more growing to do. They learn in two arenas: on the bench and in the game.

The Consultant's Loom

Healthy ministry teams deliberately cultivate and look for NEXT leaders. Whether it be a formal residency program or a keen eye for emerging talent, wise teams know that the next generation of leaders must be scouted, recruited, cultivated, called, and prepared for service. Both lay and clergy leaders comprise this group, and an emerging theme in vibrant churches is a willingness to create staff teams that blend persons with theological training with those who enter leadership from the non-theological career field. Staff can provide deliberate mentoring and coaching to those who, at any age, are considering a career in a ministry setting.

The biblical story is filled with examples of young, energetic, emerging leaders being blessed by men and women who took time with them as they discerned God's call upon their life. From Samuel to Timothy, the pattern is clear: Sense a call, find those who will nurture and help you unfold the call, and then step out in faith on your vocational journey. Strong ministry teams are always aware of that narrative and seeking to inspire their constituents to join them as they live out their life story.

NEAR Leaders:
Coaching from Experience on the Firing Line

NEAR leaders coach NOW, NEW, and NEXT leaders. NEAR leaders relate as helpers, waiting just off-stage to assist those who are in the spotlight. NEAR leaders fill defined roles—coaches, mentors, and consultants—when invited. Informally they also function as guides, scouts, and older siblings.

What the NEAR leaders provide depends on what other leaders require. They stay positioned to provide just-in-time perspective as needed. They bring lots of seasoned "been there, done that" experience to the fray.

When called, NEAR leaders move alongside current leaders as "thought partners" and "guides on the side." NEAR leaders are unique partners and resource persons for congregations' leader teams.

Partnering and teaming are common images in the New Testament, especially in Paul's writings. Paul uses lots of "we-with" language to demonstrate our partnership with God and other congregational leaders. With other leaders we are fellow workers (Rom. 16:21, Col. 4:11), fellow servants (Col. 1:7, 4:7), fellow soldiers (Phil. 2:25), and even fellow prisoners (Rom. 16:7). We're linked to other leaders and co-missioned with them. Leadership is relational, and relationships are co-created by partners.

After his resurrection Jesus served as a NEAR leader on the Emmaus road. In those encounters the people Jesus met made breakthrough discoveries that reshaped their lives and futures. Paul's ministry was full of NEAR leader actions—his letters and visits to churches and leaders (Romans 16). The books of 1, 2, and 3 John have the flavor of a wise elder leader who wrote and counseled others to seize their time on stage and to lead with boldness.

At this ministry stage I serve as a leader coach. It's satisfying to walk with other leaders—whether NOW, NEW, or NEXT—as a thought partner. Done well, we both learn and grow.

Notes

[1] Stephen R. Covey, *The 7 Habits of Highly Effective Leaders* (New York: Free Press, 1989), 232.

[2] Ronald A. Heifetz, *Leadership Without Easy Answers* (Cambridge, MA: Belknap/Harvard University Press, 1994).

[3] Susan Beaumont, "Next Generation Leaders," *Leading Ideas*, the Lewis Center, www.churchleadership.com, accessed 24 February 2016.

Down, Up, Together
Practicing a NOW-NEW-NEXT-NEAR Mix

Wise congregations are deliberate and thoughtful about the mix of their leadership. Traditional models often fail to take into account the insights, dimensions, and impacts of the NOW-NEW-NEXT-NEAR concept.

How does the NOW-NEW-NEXT-NEAR mix work in ministry practice? What happens in a well-woven team? Here's an actual case study to show how this model works.

Strong Leaders in Action

First Church is a traditional congregation that has a rich history in its community. After operating from a programmatic, staff-driven, attractional church model for many decades, the members are gradually embracing the new opportunities that adding a missional emphasis to their vision has brought them. At the same time that they are shifting their model of ministry, their staff has undergone significant changes and realignments over the last decade.

For many years the members of the ministerial staff looked very much alike, shared very similar backgrounds and educations, and filled predictable roles and positions. Using a hierarchical, chain-of-command structure, the church staff ran operations much like a manufacturing facility. Their organizational chart mirrored the local industry models, and their narrowly defined job assignments created clear silos of programs and subgroups. Efficiency was paramount, and interaction with one another was limited.

Laity were seen as implementers of the programs staff members created or imported. Ministers were viewed as the "experts" at doing church, while laypersons were the "amateurs" who provided support, encouragement, and funding as the clergy directed.

As ministers moved off the scene, the congregation recruited replacements from a vast pool of denominational-approved seminaries to take their place. The denomination made most programmatic decisions, and so the clergy proved to be relatively interchangeable and easily replaced components of a larger machine of ministry.

As the American religious culture began shifting during the last third of the 20th century, the staffing model began to show cracks and stresses as

First Church attempted to adapt to the changing landscape. Denominational decline and the demise of programmatic success meant the pipeline of formulaic tools no longer worked as hoped. The oversupply of new clergy began to dry up. Laypersons began to assert their voice in strategic decisions and to question motives, direction, and the quality of their church's ministry.

In response, members of First Church began to rethink several dimensions of their leadership culture and made four shifts:

1. They admitted that a program-driven, siloed model was increasingly ineffective and counterproductive.
2. They reconsidered the false dichotomy that led to clergy and laity working in separate "lanes" rather than collaboratively.
3. They realized that they would need to become increasingly responsible for recruiting, training, and educating their future leaders. Their homogenous team needed to give way to a team that represented the rich diversity of their congregation and community.
4. They recognized that as a church in a post-Christian 21st century culture, they must seek a better balance between their former primarily internal focus and an emerging external focus.

As a result, over the course of a decade, the leaders at First Church have gradually come to embrace several features that resonate with the themes of this book.

Calling Out NEXT Leaders

First Church has become very deliberate about calling out NEXT leaders. From middle and high school youth to collegians and adults in the midst of careers, leaders frequently suggest that vocational ministry is a viable and fulfilling option for their people.

Since elevating this conversation, several collegians and three young professionals have decided to pursue ministry or missions as a career. Others have begun to proactively volunteer at local nonprofits and ministries as part of their emerging understanding of a missional lifestyle. Small groups regularly meet to talk about the implications of integrating their faith and their work in a seamless lifestyle. Older (NOW and NEAR leaders) mentors are often asked to walk alongside adolescents or young adults who are contemplating vocational dilemmas or choices.

An emerging theme in the leadership culture of First Church is the need to cultivate, call out, and nurture the next generation of leadership for the church, both lay and clergy.

Changing Staffing Practices

First Church has shifted toward placing a higher value upon emotional intelligence and the ability of new staff to integrate and work collaboratively with others. No longer content to simply hire highly skilled individuals, leaders employ tools and methodologies that explore character and teamwork skills as well as intelligence and technical ability.

The result is an emerging collaborative spirit that undergirds nearly every ministry of the church. Vertical walls between ministries and individuals have given way to collaborative methods that emphasize the utilization of talents and gifts, regardless of position title.

Establishing a Residency Program

Through a special grant a ministry residence program has been instituted in which NEXT leaders with a seminary or divinity school degree serve a two-year residency in pastoral leadership. Much like a medical residency following medical school, this model exposes the new graduate to a wide array of ministry experiences and opportunities.

NOW clergy leaders spend time debriefing and coaching these NEXT leaders as they seek to integrate their theological training on the ground in the life of a living, breathing congregation. Additionally, collegiate students with an interest in ministry serve as interns during the academic year and/or summer break.

These NEXT leaders are cultivated and encouraged as they make their initial explorations of ministry as a vocational possibility. Plans exist to extend this ministry opportunity to upperclassmen in the local high schools who have shown a propensity and/or interest in ministry as a vocation. Nurturing their sense of call is becoming a primary initiative of the youth ministry at First Church.

Emphasizing Every Christian's Call

There is an emerging theme in all of First Church that emphasizes the "call" of every Christ-follower and the implications of that call for vocation and work. A regular theme is heard throughout the church that one's job / task / role in life is an integral part of that person's mission in life. In many ways the conversations about call that were once reserved for clergy exclusively are now permeating adult Sunday School classes, small groups, teams, and committees.

Several retired (NEAR) lay leaders are taking the initiative, alongside key peak career leaders (NOW), to cultivate this integration of faith and work among the men and women who make up the laity of First Church. Monthly fellowships are organized by career type (educational, legal, medical, corporate, etc.), and the resulting conversations between NOW-NEW-NEXT-NEAR leaders have proven to be rich and revealing.

Ministering Outside the Church Walls

Many of the changes in the leadership culture have sought to engage a growing percentage of the congregation in ministry outside the walls of the traditional church. An increasing amount of lay and clergy energy and attention is given to the community/city and its unique and complex needs.

Shifting from a funding source to a full partner in mission and ministry has necessitated new learnings from all parts of the leadership culture. Clergy must learn to be brokers and facilitators as well as participants. NEW leaders are recruited with an eye toward their ability to plant one foot firmly in the surrounding community, as well as upon the church property.

Incorporating NEXT Leaders

The senior (NOW) leaders of the church, both lay and clergy, are constantly exploring ways to innovate and incorporate the ideas and energy of younger (NEXT) colleagues. Rather than viewing the emerging new trends as threats, established leaders are providing examples as they open themselves up to new thoughts, methods, and technologies.

Including Retirees

A deliberate inclusion of retirees (NEAR leaders) is becoming standard practice at First Church. As staff members retire, they are recruited back into roles of advisors, mentors, and guides for the current (NOW) and emerging

(NEXT) leader core. In addition, they are invited into mentoring relationships with those considering ministry or church leadership roles for the first time (NEXT). The resulting relationships and connections are remarkable and have come to be highly prized by all.

One retiree served on a contract basis in pastoral care. Another was named "theologian in residence." The former pastor provided leadership for the emerging missions division of the church. In each case the NEAR leaders were clear that they were not vying or competing with the NOW leaders. As a result of these ministry partnerships, a rare synergy of wisdom paired with energy and imagination has emerged and the church is flourishing.

Owning the Church's Vision and Mission

The NOW leaders take seriously their call to be stewards of the vision and mission of the church. They pull together key lay leaders (NOW) and emerging lay leaders (NEXT) as they pray, dream, and plan the future of First Church. Focusing upon that task has meant that other NOW leaders, many of them laity, have emerged to cover tasks previously reserved for those in the pastoral role. Pastoral care of the congregation is now provided by a wide array of lay and ministerial teams who coordinate their efforts. The result is a much more responsive, available, and consistent delivery of pastoral care to those with pressing physical, spiritual, or emotional needs.

Establishing a Leadership School

Each year First Church hosts a leadership school for laity and clergy who wish to deepen their faith and/or explore the deeper dimensions of their efforts to identify their spiritual gifts and use them for the good of the Kingdom. Increasingly, awareness of spiritual gifts and an appreciation for the diversity of talents and abilities in the body are becoming a signature component of the leadership culture of First Church.

The lessons from this discussion of NOW-NEW-NEXT-NEAR leaders are exponential. The church of the 21st and 22nd centuries will need to give serious attention to leadership cultivation, training, calling, and enhancement. Learning from others who journey along this same path is an important and valuable tool in that process.

There's the leadership tapestry. Grow down, up, and then together. Ready?

The Consultant's Loom

Bob, I love this image of a fully-orbed leadership team. Is it possible for congregations and other organizations to deliberately seek to create such a leadership culture? Could it be that some of our persistent issues can be traced to a limited model of leadership?

Too often we assume that all leaders look alike and come from a similar age or demographic group. Based on my observations of healthy leadership cultures, they are more diverse than they are homogenous. Illustrating the genius of 1 Corinthians 12, effective leadership teams bring together diverse and unique individuals to accomplish together what cannot be done alone.

I hope to use your model of "Growing Leader Clusters" to evaluate the leadership teams of churches with whom our organization works. I believe we can make a case for being more proactive and deliberate in putting together teams that mirror this healthy diversity.

As part of the spiritual discernment process, we continue to learn and employ the willingness to adopt "holy indifference" as a guiding dream for the future. Growing so engaged by God's dream for us that we gradually lose sight of our own agendas is not just an exercise for the mystics, but for everyone who claims to be a Christ-follower. By doing so, we recognize that none of us have all the skills needed for any situation. We are all partial leaders in need of the other parts of the team to make up a whole. At the center of it all is the Spirit of Christ, who weaves us into a beautiful tapestry that includes and enhances all our disparate parts.

I hope everyone who reads this material has an opportunity to integrate their own gifts with those of others to collectively accomplish something no one person could do alone. This would result in gaining a taste of what God's design for the church and ministry surely must be.

Weaving in Loose Ends
Final Thoughts on Leadership

As persons and leaders, our lives work best with a minimum of loose ends. Clear beliefs and personal maturity can help turn those loose ends into added sturdy threads for living and leading. At the end of this book, here's our final chance to tie up some of those loose ends, weaving them firmly into our lives and leadership.

Throughout these pages we've woven a leadership tapestry. Lengthwise, we wove the tapestry's base from strong, undergirding theological threads for leaders. These threads go deep and give faith leaders stabilizing foundations and anchors. Then we added the cross-threads of maturity as growth and self-definition sort themselves out across leaders' lifespans. These threads provide texture, beauty, and wisdom. Together in practice, these threads create sturdy and intentional leaders—individual leaders.

Individual leaders are important but never enough. Communities rely on their leaders to set the pace, and those leaders need communities to influence. Community leadership's collaboration really does "take a village." Why? Because lasting community transformation takes all of us doing our best work and growing together.

So, in this book we moved finally from the individual leader to multiples of leaders. We explored how NOW, NEW, NEXT, and NEAR leaders team up to create powerful and effective blends of experience and strength. With theological clarity and a variety of life stages and leader gifts interlaced, we wove together working teams with greater balance and flexibility. We advocated communities of leaders for communities of practice.

Expanding Theological Strands

We often discover God more clearly amid life's breakthroughs and breakdowns. When we're in unfamiliar territory God uses our uncertainty to tie up some of our loose ends and to deepen our root systems.

It's telling that Paul's term for discernment means "to sift." When new situations face us, spiritual sifting and sorting become both necessities and opportunities. Here are just a few "loose end" turning points for our theological growth:

When God "Grows" Inside Us

Sometimes our lives bring us to crossroads where God is suddenly bigger or vastly different than we'd realized before. Maybe you have a "Jonah experience" when you discover the people you hate are loved by God. Or, maybe the warmth of human love breaks into your heart, and your God morphs from being a celestial cop to a caring friend and then to a grace-full God.

In a classic book by J. B. Philips, he raised a pivotal question: Is your God too small?[1] Maybe there's a bigger question for you: Is your God big enough for you now? When our experience with God enlarges and becomes more profound, we grow down as well as growing up.

- ☐ When has your view of God "grown" and caused your beliefs to expand too?
- ☐ When has the enlarged "size" of your God challenged your faith and theology to grow?
- ☐ How has a "larger God" changed your life and leadership?

When We See Our Future More Clearly

The future captures our imaginations. It's no wonder the happenings on the Transfiguration Mount opened the disciples' eyes wide. What began as a simple prayer retreat quickly became a milestone event, a foretaste of the future, and a miracle that happened to Jesus himself. In that event Peter, James, and John met prophets from the past and heard words about Jesus' future "departure" (Luke 9:31). Together, the inner circle of disciples stood for a moment on a bridge between earth and heaven, between the past and future. The impact on the disciples was transformative and lasting. Later, John recalled seeing Jesus' "glory" (John 1:14), and Peter described his "greatness" (2 Pet. 1:16-18).

Those rare moments when God gives us a glimpse of the future are life-changers and belief-expanders. Think about those high-impact events and how they've challenged to you.

- ☐ When have you seen God in a larger, longer frame?
- ☐ How have glimpses of your future opened new vistas for you?

When Grace Gets Our Attention

Each of us has needed to be rescued at some point, haven't we? Jesus' best-known story was a 911 call (Luke 15:11-32). A traveler had been robbed, beaten, and abandoned. He was desperate for a neighborly helping hand. "Good" people hurried past without aiding the wounded traveler. Then, a hated Samaritan became "good" when he stopped, helped, and guaranteed the traveler's care.

Luke, the only Gentile writer in the New Testament, had keen eyes for good Samaritans, outcasts, females, and the poor in his gospel account. Challenging traditional views of who was included and excluded, Luke spotlighted God showing grace and care for these marginalized persons. When God's grace surprises us, our theology expands to match God's reach.

- ☐ When has God's love surprised you?
- ☐ When have you been blessed beyond hope?
- ☐ How has grace transformed your beliefs and behaviors?

When We Can't Escape Our Prejudices

In the Old Testament Jonah was described as a reluctant, half-hearted missionary. He first ran from God and the divine call to minister to Nineveh, his hated enemy. Winds, waves, and whales got Jonah's full attention. When under duress he finally went to Nineveh, his sermon was one short, bitter sentence (Jon. 3:4). Then, with his warning delivered, he retreated to a vantage point to watch with glee while God wiped out the entire city.

But the fire didn't fall. Instead, Jonah's message was heard and heeded. Nineveh repented, turned to God, and was spared. As a result, Jonah exploded in anger. He was mad at both a gracious God and a repentant Nineveh. He decided he would rather die than live in his expanded world. Maybe he never got the point. The book of Jonah ends with God asking a powerful question about the nature of God: "Should not I pity Nineveh?" (Jon. 4:11). We don't hear a response from Jonah.

God gave Jonah a living demonstration of second chances for Jonah and Nineveh. God gave Jonah a prime opportunity to expand his theology and worldview significantly: Could Jonah embrace an everybody, every-where, everytime God? We're left to wonder: Did Jonah ever see beyond his pre-shrunk deity?

Leaders aren't spared from prejudice. We all have people and situations we have pre-judged. We face these circumstances on spiritual auto-pilot and don't see the narrowed condition of our hearts. Our blindness blocks us from seeing God's grace and love, as the redemptive giver of second chances.

- [ ]   When have you faced your prejudices?
- [ ]   When has your dark side been brought into light?
- [ ]   How have you seen the world through God's eyes?

When Feedback Opens New Horizons for Us

At first blush Job's "friends" weren't very helpful, were they? They judged him more than they supported him. That's not all bad. Comfort zones don't host growth spurts. Feedback that causes us to ask deeper questions and to look for fresh answers is most apt to trigger growth in us.

Just as Job's woes were a "test case," so is some feedback. "Friendly" feedback—even if some ideas aren't accurate—can open our minds and souls to personal discoveries. Having fresh questions to explore and to answer helps us find new pathways and potentials.

- [ ]   When has feedback helped you grow?
- [ ]   Who gives you high-impact feedback?
- [ ]   How do you move beyond your resistance to feedback?

What other soul-expanders have opened your eyes and heart to God at work in you? We've only offered a short list of theological loose ends for you to explore and tie up. Add your experiences to these theological turning points. Most importantly, continue to keep your beliefs growing. As good gardeners know and practice, what you plant and cultivate, you will harvest.

Healing Maturity's Stretch Marks

When life stretches us we don't go back to the same size. The stretches leave room for maturity and its unique stretch marks. As an example, trees' growth rings show the marks of severe droughts and big forest fires. Our growth spurts are often triggered by tough challenges.

- [ ]   When have you matured most?
- [ ]   What triggered your most significant changes?
- [ ]   How have you matured from your stretch marks?

Following are just a few stretch marks that invite us to grow and mature:

When We Get Stuck in a Life Stage

Sometimes we don't master the challenges of our current life stage and aren't ready for our next stage, and therefore get "stuck in a stage." This loss of psychological traction and the accompanying sense of being stuck limits our forward movement and maturation.

In the "launch" decades' chapter we noted that some athletes and entertainers peak early, experience lots of success as very young people, slide past some challenges of youthful life stages, and miss mastering some necessary emotional hurdles. As they age, these early-peaking adults experience their own unique type of "generation gap." They may struggle later in life when their psychological gaps "catch up" with them.

Scripture brims over with leaders who had to grow up and grow down over time. Joseph moved beyond a favored child who flaunted his "coat of many colors" to his brothers. After prison he rescued his family from famine and preserved their future (Genesis 35–50). As a young person John Mark abandoned Paul's first missionary journey (Acts 13:13-14), but he grew up and became valuable to Paul's later ministry (2 Tim. 4:11). John matured beyond his early title, a "son of thunder" (Mark 3:16-17), to become a seasoned elder who wrote to his "little children" and reminded believers to love one another (1 John 2:12-29).

- ☐ How alert are you to the unique challenges of your current life stage?
- ☐ How aware are you of any lessons from earlier stages you may have failed to learn?
- ☐ What have you learned as you've caught up with lessons you didn't master during earlier life stages?

When Our Birthright Gets Misplaced

In the Bible and into feudal history firstborn children received special favor through a birthright. The law of primogeniture ("first to be born") granted the legacy of family leadership along with the family estate to the firstborn son. In many family lines now the blessing is passed along smoothly and without fanfare. But in other cases the gift of the birthright gets complicated.

Remember the Genesis' birthright saga of twin brothers, Jacob and Esau? Their competition had begun in the womb when Jacob grabbed his twin's heel in a futile effort to be born first. But Esau was the firstborn, and the competitive relationship deepened beyond the twins to include their parents. Father Isaac loved Esau, while Mother Rebekah loved Jacob (Gen. 25:28).

Rebekah and Jacob conspired and succeeded in capturing Esau's birthright. Jacob's lineage, then, formed the Jews, while Esau's children became the Muslims—and that religious and cultural competition continues to this day.

Birthrights are still given or withheld. As I mentioned earlier, the Dale family birthright was lost in World War II when my dad's older brother was killed in action. The loss of the golden child meant my dad received no blessing to pass along. In Old Testament studies during my mid-20s I realized my blessing would have to come from two sources: my mother's family and directly from God. It was a freeing discovery, because it removed a frustratingly blind quest for a birthright blessing that wasn't there to be bestowed.

Blessings are precious gifts to receive. Then, they are to be paid forward. We may count our blessings with grateful hearts, but then we pass them along with grace.

☐   How have blessings been passed along in your life?
☐   When has competition for blessings become a barrier for you?
☐   Who has blessed you for your future?
☐   Whom are you blessing?

When Trauma Teaches Tough Lessons

Tragedies and losses leave their scars on our psyches and challenge us to grow beyond our negative experiences. Human scar tissue is tougher than regular skin, but it's also less sensitive. Lower sensitivity makes our traumas potential emotional divides. Have your traumas made you more teachable and more mature? Or, have your traumas just toughened you and left you less sensitive?

Thankfully, in many cases trauma can become a transformative teacher. In the Old Testament the Hebrews carried the scars of captivity in Egypt on their bodies and in their hearts far beyond the Red Sea. As a result they defended the widow, cared for the orphan, and sheltered the traveling stranger who appeared at their doors (Deut. 10:18). Concern for the alienated and defenseless became a consistent practice for the Hebrews. Then, in the New Testament, Jesus made these actions of the heart a watershed in the Last Judgment. Additionally, Jesus added other scarred faces to the list of traumatized ones: the hungry, the thirsty, the naked, the sick, and the prisoner (Matt. 25:31-46).

Trauma may stop life in its tracks. Trauma, then, becomes an opportunity for us to grow up. More maturity may encourage us to help others who are also in difficult circumstances. Because of the scars of Egypt, the faithful have over time created orphanages, hospitals, and hotels. We have the option to mature or not when we face life's hurdles.

☐ How have your psychic scars sensitized you?
☐ How are you more grown up as a result of your traumas?

When Birth Order's Advantages Undercut Us

There's an ironic rule in human development: Any strength, when overused, becomes a weakness. When we rely too much on an obvious gift, two problems can emerge: We may become a "one note" specialist and lose our versatility, or we may neglect to cultivate our lesser talents and become weighed down by their weakness.

That asset-liability imbalance is a common pattern in birth order. First-borns are typically responsible torchbearers for their families, but they may take on too much, over-function, and burn out. Middle-borns are often family mediators, diplomats, and harmonizers, but they may become so concerned with others that they neglect self-care. Last-borns are usually independent operators, but they may act entitled and not cooperative. In each case, assets can morph into liabilities. Mature leaders find ways to steward their strengths while guarding against their weaknesses.

☐ What strengths have you overused and, as a result, weakened yourself?
☐ How are you using strengths from your birth order?
☐ How are you overcoming any weaknesses of your birth order?

A friend tells me he intends to still be growing at his death. He describes his goal as staying "green above the ears." Maybe that's the way to keep on maturing: to open yourself to more growth at every life stage. Go for it. Make all of your milestones future ones.

Teams on Trial

The final proof of the leadership loom is effective practice. Teams are the proof in the pudding. With teams, challenges are overcome and opportunities seized.

When "Leader" Is Only Singular

Today's leadership situations are often too complex for isolated leaders to master. Two or three or four heads are better than one. In earlier eras the Great Man theory of leadership reigned. Pioneers and lone rangers were popular.

But we now live in a global network of challenges and barriers. Cooperation beats competition every time. It's an era that demands spelling "leader" with plurals. Co-leadership makes sense in our day.[2]

When Today Overlooks Tomorrow

A new study of 18 leaders in high-profile corporate and sports roles shows that "super-leaders"[3] prepare others to step into key roles. "Coaching trees" depict how some sports coaches nurture those who succeed next. Remarkably, in 2008, 26 of the 32 head coaches in the National Football League had been trained by Bill Walsh, the late coach of the San Francisco 49ers.

Walsh had the knack of giving personalized attention to his assistants, bringing out their best, developing their creativity, and encouraging them to adapt fearlessly to new challenges. Walsh perfected the West Coast Offense, but he's remembered even more for the leaders he launched. Tomorrow was on his horizon each day. As a NOW leader, Walsh looked for NEW and NEXT leaders and developed them for the future.

The Consultant's Loom

We hope you have heard clearly that the path to effective leadership is a lifelong journey. None of us come into our leadership roles with all the tools we need for the task. All of us have areas of strength, natural giftedness, blind spots, and mixed agendas. We are a mass of contradictions and easily lured off course by our imperfections. The loose ends we describe here exist in everyone and for all of life. Wise leaders acknowledge our flaws like the Navajo weavers. We lean into the possibilities rather than living in denial.

One of the finest leaders I know is always the first one to tell me of the new book he has read, the new insight he has gained, or the new revelation God has placed in his heart and mind. From a distance he looks like the finished product and has many people who sing his praises. He is universally admired as one of the brightest, most insightful people any of us know.

As a good friend I get to see "behind the curtain," and there I find someone who is humbly aware of and willing to admit how much he doesn't know. Part of what makes him so successful is his willingness to admit his own loose ends. He spends little time pointing out the shortcomings of others, but is always willing to turn the spotlight of inspection upon his own life and to make whatever adjustments seem necessary.

This is the biblical model of a growing, effective leader. Humility, tied to honesty before God and others, coupled with a strong desire to bring glory to God and not self is at the heart of powerful leadership.

If you want to continue your journey toward becoming the person and leader God intended you to be, you will find yourself in a memorable company of sisters and brothers who share the same quest. Remember the lesson of Exodus 18:18, "You cannot do this alone." Find others to join you in your path toward becoming the leader God intends you to be. Whether a coach, colleague, mentor, or friend, you will benefit from their insights, questions, probing, and encouragement. You, in turn, will find yourself invited into such relationships with others, and will discover the great joy of being the encourager as well as the encouraged.

You're at the leadership loom now. Identify your strong theological threads. Then bring your textured maturity threads to the loom. Weave them together for strength and beauty. Cultivate your inner strengths.

Now, lead from them. Keep on growing down and up. Keep on growing together and working with other gifted leaders, and weaving. It's your leadership opportunity.

Your Own Thought Partner

Would a free personalized coaching session help you begin to weave your own "grow down, grow up, grow together" process into a stronger expression of you as a leader?

If so, contact us for a 30-minute coaching conversation. The Center for Healthy Churches will provide you with an initial conversation about how you might benefit from having a leadership coach walk with you along the path toward a greater awareness of your leadership potential. Email us at contact@chchurches.org to start that journey. We're ready to start when you're ready to grow.

Notes

[1] J. B. Phillips, *Your God Is Too Small: A Guide to Believers and Skeptics Alike* (New York: Macmillan, 1953).

[2] David Al Heenan and Warren Bennis, *Co-Leaders: The Power of Great Partnerships* (New York: John Wiley, 1999).

[3] Sydney Finkelstein, *Superbosses: How Exceptional Leaders Master the Flow of Talent* (New York: Portfolio/Penguin, 2016).

CPSIA information can be obtained
at www.ICGtesting.com
Printed in the USA
LVOW13s1446190517
534923LV00011B/123/P

9 781635 280005